Pocket
MIAMI
TOP SIGHTS • LOCAL LIFE • MADE EASY

Regis St Louis

In This Book

QuickStart Guide

Your keys to understanding the city – we help you decide what to do and how to do it

Need to Know
Tips for a smooth trip

Neighborhoods
What's where

Explore Miami

The best things to see and do, neighborhood by neighborhood

Top Sights
Make the most of your visit

Local Life
The insider's city

The Best of Miami

The city's highlights in handy lists to help you plan

Best Walks
See the city on foot

Miami's Best...
The best experiences

Survival Guide

Tips and tricks for a seamless, hassle-free city experience

Getting Around
Travel like a local

Essential Information
Including where to stay

Our selection of the city's best places to eat, drink and experience:

◉ **Sights**

✖ **Eating**

▣ **Drinking**

✿ **Entertainment**

⊡ **Shopping**

These symbols give you the vital information for each listing:

☑	Telephone Numbers	♦	Family-Friendly
⊙	Opening Hours	❀	Pet-Friendly
Ⓟ	Parking	⛵	Bus
⊖	Nonsmoking	⛴	Ferry
@	Internet Access	Ⓜ	Metro
⧉	Wi-Fi Access	Ⓢ	Subway
⚲	Vegetarian Selection	Ⓣ	Tram
⊡	English-Language Menu	Ⓡ	Train

Find each listing quickly on maps for each neighborhood:

Bar Hemingway

16 ▣ Map p233, B2

Legend has it that Hemi self, wielding a machine ...rate this timber-pane ...ered bar during ... showpiece is a ...en by Papa a... town. Dress ...s.com; Hôtel Rit ⊙6.30pm-2a

6 ◉ Plac Ve...

The Best of Miami 127

Miami's Best Walks

Miami's Best ...

Survival Guide 147

QuickStart Guide

Welcome to Miami

Sun-kissed beaches and art-deco beauties make an alluring backdrop to Miami's many charms, starting with the city's burgeoning arts scene. It's a place where creativity reins supreme: in its open-air galleries of street art, globally inspired restaurants and packed festival calendar. Add in a healthy dose of Latin culture, steamy beach days and hedonistic nightlife, and you have one of America's most captivating cities.

South Beach (p32)
MIAMI2YOU/SHUTTERSTOCK ©

Miami
Top Sights

Art Deco Historic District (p26)
America's most captivating art-deco district.

LITTLENY/SHUTTERSTOCK ©

Wynwood Walls (p74)

A jaw-dropping collection of street art.

Pérez Art Museum Miami (p54)

Miami's epicenter of contemporary art.

Vizcaya Museum & Gardens (p102)

European palace on Biscayne Bay.

Adrienne Arsht Center for the Performing Arts (p56)

Miami's top performing arts hall.

Bayfront Park (p58)
Downtown Miami's waterfront park.

Fairchild Tropical Garden (p114)
South Florida's most beautiful gardens.

Biltmore Hotel (p116)
Architectural beauty from the 1920s.

Miami
Local Life

*Local experiences and hidden gems
to help you uncover the real city*

There's much more to Miami than just its beautiful beaches. This is a city of cutting-edge design, hallowed art galleries and lush islands just beyond the city center. Exploring Miami's diverse neighborhoods is one of the great rewards of a trip

Indie Shops of South Beach (p28)

☑ Eye-catching boutiques ☑ Decadent snacking and sipping

Art & High Design (p76)

☑ Surreal public art ☑ Jewel-box storefronts

Downtown & Brickell (p60)

☑ Rooftop views ☑ Urban exploring

BARRY WINKER/GETTY IMAGES ©

Wandering the Grove (p104)
☑ Waterfront oases ☑ Indie cafes and bars

FOTOLUMINATE LLC/SHUTTERSTOCK ©

Key Biscayne (p90)
☑ Seaside adventures ☑ Panoramic dining

ROSA IRENE BETANCOURT 7 / ALAMY STOCK PHOTO ©

Other great places to experience the city like a local:

Outdoor Screenings (p38)

South Pointe Park (p36)

Secret Garden (p35)

Keeping it Kosher (p51)

A Farm-to-Table Dinner (p67)

Boxelder (p86)

Monthly Art Fest (p82)

Iconic Cinema (p96)

Art & Song (p111)

Japanese Cuisine (p123)

The Upper East Side (p88)
☑ Neighborhood Parks ☑ Poolside Drinks

Miami
Day Planner

Day One

Start the day with a morning stroll along the lovely shoreline of South Beach. Afterwards, stop in the small **Art Deco Museum** (p32) for an overview of this fabulous architectural district. Then take a wander along Ocean Drive and see these deco beauties in person.

Have a seafood lunch at **Joe's Stone Crab Restaurant** (p37). Afterwards, take a stroll along Lincoln Rd, a pedestrian boulevard lined with eye-catching stores and outdoor restaurants. Peruse fiction at **Books & Books** (p42), pick up some beach footwear at **Havaianas** (p42) and browse eye-catching apparel at **Alchemist** (p29).

In the evening, feast on high-end Southern fare at **Yardbird** (p36). Catch a show at the **Fillmore Miami Beach** (p41) or a concert at the **New World Center** (p32). End the night over at **Bodega** (p38), a taco stand with a decadent bar hidden out the back. For something a little more raucous, join the party over at **Mango's** (p38).

Day Two

Begin the day in Wynwood over pastries from **Salty Donut** (p81) and espresso from **Panther Coffee** (p82). Thus fortified, begin the gallery and shopping stroll of this fascinating neighborhood. Check out the latest murals at **Wynwood Walls** (p74), look for gifts at **Malaquita** (p87) and explore the outstanding installations at the **Margulies Collection at the Warehouse** (p80).

Spend the afternoon at the **Pérez Art Museum Miami** (p54), which has some of the best contemporary art exhibitions in the city – plus a great lunch spot. Afterwards, head over to **Bayfront Park** (p61) to check out a few Noguchi sculptures, and join locals for a bit of riverside relaxing on the grass.

That evening, return to Wynwood to see the district by lamplight. Book a table at culinary hot spot **Kyu** (p83), check out the microbrew scene at **Wynwood Brewing Company** (p85), then take in a band in the backyard of **Gramps** (p86), the **Wynwood Yard** (p85) or **Lagniappe** (p84). If you're still out late, join the party people at DJ-fueled **Bardot** (p85).

Short on time?

We've arranged Miami's must-sees into these day-by-day itineraries to make sure you see the very best of the city in the time you have available.

Day Three

☀ Spend the morning wandering around the lush grounds and art- and antique-filled interiors of **Vizcaya Museum & Gardens** (p102). Next, go over to Coconut Grove for window shopping and snacks (try the ice cream from **Bianco Gelato**, p105). Take a peak at **Barnacle Historic State Park** (p105) for waterfront views, then have lunch at **the Spillover** (p109).

☀ Head to Little Havana for a dose of Latin culture. Check out the domino action in **Máximo Gómez Park** (p95), learn a bit of Cuban history at **Cuban Memorial Park** (p95) and shop for *guayaberas* (Cuban dress shirts) and cigars along 8th St. Stop for a freshly squeezed pick-me-up at **Los Pinareños Frutería** (p97).

☾ Have an early dinner at the Cuban icon **Versailles** (p96). Afterwards, go to the intimate **Cuboocho** (p98), where you can hear Latin jazz, flamenco, Cuban son, and other styles. For something more spirited, head over to the long-running **Ball & Chain** (p97), which has a full calendar of events and music (including salsa – with free lessons – on some nights).

Day Four

☀ Explore Miami's wilder side at the **Fairchild Tropical Garden** (p114), with its rainforest sections, colorful butterflies and pretty woodland paths. After a dose of nature, go up to Coral Gables for a stroll along shop-lined Miracle Mile. Learn about this curious master-planned village at the **Coral Gables Museum** (p121).

☀ Stop in for a flat white and creative lunch specials at **Threefold** (p122). If the weather is steamy, head over to the **Venetian Pool** (p120) for a dip in one of America's loveliest swimming spots. Otherwise, opt for the **Biltmore Hotel** (p116) for a wander through a grand building modeled on Seville's Giralda Tower. Be sure to have a drink at the elegant poolside restaurant.

☾ Head downtown for an early seafood feast at the always lively **River Oyster Bar** (p67). Afterwards, attend a show at the Adrienne Arsht Center for the Performing Arts. Be sure to check out the subtle art designs (by José Bedia) on the inside. Cap the night with drinks at a Downtown rooftop bar such as **Sugar** (p61), **Area 31** (p68) or **Pawnbroker** (p69).

Need to Know

**For more information,
see Survival Guide (p147)**

Currency
US dollars ($)

Language
English, Spanish

Visas
Required for most foreign visitors unless
eligible for the Visa Waiver Program.

Money
ATMs are widely available, though most ATM
withdrawals using out-of-state cards incur
surcharges of $3 or so. Major credit cards are
widely accepted.

Cell Phones
Local SIM cards can be used in European or
Australian phones. Europe and Asia's GSM
900/1800 standard is incompatible with the
USA's cell-phone systems. Check with your
service provider about using your phone in the US.

Time
Eastern Time (GMT/UTC minus five hours)

Tipping
Tipping is standard practice across America. In
restaurants, tipping 15 to 20% of the bill is expected;
only tip below this if the service was exceptionally
bad (not tipping is a very drastic move). For food a tip
for normal service is 15%, good service is 18% and
great service is 20%. At bars, it's $1 per drink or $2
or more for complicated cocktails. Taxi drivers get
tipped 10-15% of the fare, while porters and
skycaps get $1 a bag. For hotel cleaning staff, a
few dollars after a few nights should suffice.

① Before You Go

Your Daily Budget

Budget: Less than $150
► Hostel dorms: $30–50
► Meal from a food truck: $10
► Happy hour drink special: from $5

Midrange: $150–$300
► Standard hotel room: $150–250
► Midrange dinner: $30–50
► Craft cocktail in a lounge: $12–16

Top End: More than $300
► Cover at nightclubs: from $20
► Dinner at upscale restaurants: from $60
► Day at the spa: from $150

Useful Websites

Miami (www.miamiandbeaches.com) Excellent gateway to neighborhoods, restaurants, nightlife and events.

New Times (www.miaminewtimes.com/restaurants) Art openings, concerts and restaurant and nightlife reviews.

Miami Nice (www.miaminicemag.com) Local blog covering fashion, food and culture.

Miami Bites (www.miabites.com) Food bloggers share the latest hits.

Lonely Planet (www.lonelyplanet.com/miami) Destination information, hotel bookings, traveller forum and more.

Advance Planning

One month before Book tickets for big events.

Two weeks before Reserve tables at high-end restaurants.

One week before Check online for the latest restaurant and bar openings and art exhibitions.

② Arriving in Miami

✈ From Miami International Airport

Miami International Airport Taxis charge a flat rate for the 40-minute drive to South Beach ($35). The Miami Beach Airport Express (bus 150) costs $2.65 and makes stops all along Miami Beach, from 41st to the southern tip. SuperShuttle runs a shared-van service, costing about $22 to South Beach.

✈ From Fort Lauderdale-Hollywood International Airport

GO Airport Shuttle runs shared vans to Miami, with prices around $25 to South Beach. A taxi costs around $75 (metered fare) to South Beach and $65 to Downtown.

③ Getting Around

🚗 Rental Car

Convenient for getting around, but parking can be expensive. Miami drivers can be aggressive, and traffic congestion can be intense.

🚗 Taxi & Ride-Sharing Services

Handy for getting between destinations if you don't want to drive, but can be pricey for long distances. Taxis are difficult to hail on the street; call or use an app for a pick up.

🚌 Bus

Extensive system, but slow for long journeys.

Ⓜ Metromover

The Metromover, which is equal parts bus, monorail and train, is helpful for getting around Downtown Miami.

🚌 Trolley

Free service with various routes in Miami Beach, Downtown, Wynwood, Coconut Grove, Coral Gables, Little Havana and other neighborhoods. The Trolley (www.miamigov.com/trolley) is actually a hybrid-electric bus disguised as an orange and green trolley.

🚃 Train

Metrorail is a 21-mile-long heavy-rail system that has one elevated line running from Hialeah through Downtown Miami and south to Kendall/Dadeland. Pay with the reloadable Easy Card or single-use Easy Ticket, which are sold from vending machines at Metrorail stations.

The regional Tri-Rail double-decker commuter trains run the 71 miles between Dade, Broward and Palm Beach counties. Fares are calculated on a zone basis.

🚲 Citi Bike

Bike-sharing network in both Miami and Miami Beach. Easy to check out from a self-serve kiosk with a credit card. With heavy traffic, however, riding long distances can be hazardous.

Miami
Neighborhoods

Wynwood & the Design District (p72)
A hotbed of creativity, with street murals, indie boutiques and buzzing nightlife. Known for art galleries and microbreweries.

◉ Top Sight

Wynwood Walls

Little Havana (p92)
Stroll colorful Calle Ocho for a taste of Latin culture with its fine Cuban cooking, eye-catching storefronts and live music.

Coral Gables (p112)
Feels like a Mediterranean town dropped into greater Miami, with shopping on Miracle Mile, a Venetian pool and cultural theaters.

◉ Top Sights

Fairchild Tropical Garden

Biltmore Hotel

Biltmore
◉ *Hotel*

Coconut Grove (p100)
A peaceful waterfront neighborhood with tree-lined streets ripe for exploring and several gardens to visit for a nature fix.

◉ Top Sight

Vizcaya Museum & Gardens

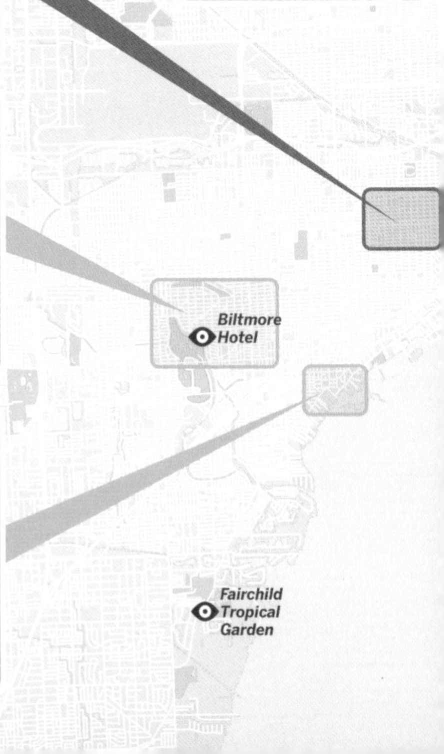

Fairchild
◉ *Tropical*
Garden

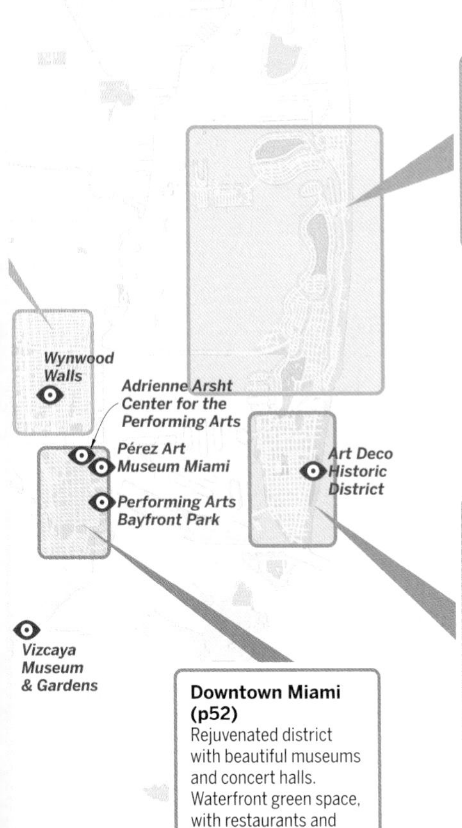

Northern Miami Beach (p44)
Home to less touristy beaches and a mangrove-filled state park. The postwar architecture hides many options for nighttime.

Wynwood Walls
◉

Adrienne Arsht Center for the Performing Arts

Pérez Art Museum Miami
◉ ◉

Performing Arts Bayfront Park
◉

Art Deco Historic District
◉

South Beach (p24)
Fabled destination for shoreline fun, nightlife and art-deco architecture, Miami Beach also has cultural sights and shopping

◉ **Top Sight**

Art Deco Historic District

◉
Vizcaya Museum & Gardens

Downtown Miami (p52)
Rejuvenated district with beautiful museums and concert halls. Waterfront green space, with restaurants and rooftop bars.

◉ **Top Sights**

Pérez Art Museum Miami

Adrienne Arsht Center for the Performing Arts

Bayfront Park

Explore
Miami

Northern Miami Beach .... `44`

Downtown Miami .... `52`

Wynwood &
the Design District .... `72`

Little Havana .... `92`

Coconut Grove .... `100`

Coral Gables .... `112`

Worth a Trip
Upper East Side...88
Key Biscayne 90

Miami skyline
SEANPAVONEPHOTO/GETTY IMAGES ©

Explore

South Beach

The most iconic neighborhood in Greater Miami, South Beach is a vertiginous landscape of sparkling beach, beautiful art-deco architecture, high-end boutiques and buzzing bars and restaurants. South Beach has its glamour, but there's more to this district than just velvet ropes and high-priced lodging. You'll find some great down-to-earth bars, good ethnic eating and excellent museums.

The Sights in a Day

☀️ Begin the day with an early-morning walk along the beachfront. Afterwards, have a healthy breakfast and a good coffee at **Dirt** (p34). Once caffeinated, hit the streets for a photo-snapping architectural stroll around the **Art Deco Historic District** (p26). Then delve deeper into art and design at the excellent **Wolfsonian-FIU** (p32).

☀️ Around lunchtime, head over to **Pubbelly** (p36) in Sunset Harbour for creative cooking with a global palate. Afterwards, check out the shops on the nearby strip – and pick up a treat for later from **True Loaf** (p28), with its astoundingly good pastries. Walk off your lunch on Lincoln Road, an appealing pedestrian strip lined with shops and cafes.

🌙 In the late afternoon, stop in for happy hour drinks and oysters at **Sweet Liberty** (p38). Catch a show at the Colony Theatre, then have a late dinner at the elegant **Yuca** (p38). Switch gears following the meal, and join the party people over at **Kill Your Idol** (p39) or **Bodega** (p38).

For a local's day in South Beach, see p32.

👁️ Top Sight

Art Deco Historic District (p26)

🔍 Local Life

Indie Shops of South Beach (p32)

💜 Best of Miami

Drinking & Nightlife
Sweet Liberty (p38)

Mango's Tropical Cafe (p38)

Eating
Yardbird (p36)

Pubbelly (p36)

Shopping
Nomad Tribe (p42)

Books & Books (p42)

Getting There

🚌 **Bus** From Downtown, bus 120 (which runs up NE 1st Ave) and bus 103 (which runs up Biscayne Blvd) head to South Beach via the MacArthur Causeway.

⛴️ **Boat** Water Taxi Miami provides ferry transport between South Beach and the Bayside Marketplace in Downtown Miami.

🚲 **Bike** The Venetian Causeway is the safest route between Miami and Miami Beach.

Top Sights
Art Deco Historic District

The world-famous Art Deco Historic District of Miami Beach is pure exuberance: architecture of bold lines, whimsical tropical motifs and a color palette that evokes all the beauty of the Miami landscape. Among the 800 deco buildings listed on the National Register of Historic Buildings, each design is different, and it's hard not to be captivated when strolling among these restored beauties from a bygone era.

👁 Map p30, E4

Ocean Dr

Cavalier hotel

Background

In 1926 a hurricane left a devastating swath across the island and much of South Florida. When it was time to rebuild, Miami Beach would undergo a dramatic rebirth, becoming the epicenter of a ground-breaking new design sweeping across Europe. Hundreds of new hotels were built during the 1930s, to accommodate the influx of middle-class tourists flooding into Miami Beach for a slice of sand and sun. The golden era of deco architecture continued until it all came to an end during WWII.

Deco Style

The building style was very much rooted in the times. The late 1920s and 1930s was an era of invention – of new automobiles, streamlined machines, radio antennae and cruise ships. Architects manifested these elements in strong lines, at times coupled with zig-zigs or sleek curves, all of which created the illusion of movement, of the bold forward march into the future.

In Miami Beach architects also incorporated more local motifs such as palm trees, flamingos and tropical plants. Nautical themes also appeared, with playful representations of ocean waves, sea horses, starfish and lighthouses. The style later became known as tropical deco.

The Best of Ocean Drive

One stretch of Ocean Dr has a collection of some of the most striking art-deco buildings in Miami Beach. Between 11th and 14th Sts, you'll see many of the classic deco elements at play in beautifully designed works – each bursting with personality. Worth noting for their stunning art deco archircture are the Congress Hotel, reminiscent of the grand movie palaces of the 1930s, the nautical-themed Tides hotel (www.tidessouthbeach.com) and the seahorse-themed Cavalier (www.cavaliersouthbeach).

☑ **Top Tips**

▶ Go early in the day when the crowds are thinnest, and the light is best for taking pictures.

▶ For deeper insight into the architecture, take a guided walking tour offered daily by the Miami Design Preservation League (p153).

▶ Complete the deco experience by checking out the excellent exhibitions at the Art Deco Museum (p32) or the Wolfsonian-FIU (p32), both nearby.

✗ **Take a Break**

Stop in for sandwiches, gelato and excellent espresso at **Pinocchio** (☏305-672-3535; 760 Ocean Dr, entrance on 8th St; mains $7-11; ⊘8am-6pm). Complete the journey into the past with a meal in the **11th St Diner** (☏305-534-6373; www.eleventhstreetdiner.com; 1065 Washington Ave; mains $10-20; ⊘7am-midnight Sun-Wed, 24hr Thu-Sat), set in a 1940s train car.

Local Life
Indie Shops of South Beach

Miami Beach's deco-loving 'hood has much more up its sleeve than just lovely hotels and buzzing nightlife. Away from Ocean Dr, palm-lined promenades and a bay-front shopping enclave draw the fashion-minded crowd of South Beach. It's not all high-priced couture though. It's the unique indie stores, as well as galleries, outdoor cafes and bakeries, that give this neighborhood so much character.

❶ True Loaf

Start the day with fresh pastries **here** (☎786-216-7207; 1894 Bay Rd; ⊙7am-6pm Mon-Sat, from 8am Sun; pastries $3-5). The best bakery in South Beach is a bread-box sized space where you can pick up heavenly croissants, tarts and kouign amman (Breton-style butter cake).

❷ Panther Coffee

Loved by locals, **Panther** (www.panther coffee.com, 1875 Purdy Ave; ⊙7am-9pm;

pastries $3-5; coffees $3-6) serves the city's best coffee, and remains little known to the Ocean Dr crowds. It has the same elegant vintage-chic vibe as its Wynwood branch and outdoor seating, plus delectable pastries to boot.

❸ Sunset Clothing Co
A great little fashion **boutique** (www.facebook.com/SunsetClothingCo; 1895 Purdy Ave; ⏱10am-8pm Mon-Sat, 11am-6pm Sun) for stylish gear that won't cost a fortune (though it isn't cheap either). You'll find well-made shirts, soft cotton T-shirts, lace-up canvas shoes, nicely fitting denim (including vintage Levi's), warm sweaters and other casual gear. Helpful friendly service, too.

❹ Maurice Gibb Memorial Park
A small bit of **greenspace** (18th St & Purdy Ave) overlooking the water, this palm-fringed park has a playground, benches and grassy areas. It's a favorite destination for dog walkers, runners, and families with kids. Against a backdrop of bobbing sailboats and the Venetian Causeway, it's worth stopping by to admire the view.

❺ Alchemist
This high-end **boutique** (☎305-531-4653; 1111 Lincoln Rd; ⏱10am-10pm) has a wild collection of artful objects, including Warhol-style soup-can candles, heavy gilded corkscrews, Beats headphones by Dr Dre, and mirrored circular sunglasses that are essential for the beach. The clothing here tends to be fairly avant-garde.

❻ Taschen
An inviting well-stocked **collection** (☎305-538-6185; www.taschen.com; 1111 Lincoln Rd; ⏱11am-9pm Mon-Thu, to 10pm Fri & Sat, noon-9pm Sun) of art, photography, design and coffee-table books to make your home look that much smarter. A couple of volumes worth browsing include David Hockney's color-rich art books and Sebastião Salgado's lushly photographed human-filled landscapes.

❼ ArtCenter/South Florida
Established in 1984 by a forward-thinking group of artists, this **compound** (☎305-674-8278; www.artcentersf.org; 2nd fl, 924 Lincoln Rd; ⏱11am-7pm Mon-Fri, noon-8pm Sat & Sun) is the creative heart of South Beach. In addition to some 52 artists' studios (many open to the public), ArtCenter offers an exciting lineup of classes and lectures. The residences are reserved for artists who do not have major exposure, so this is a good place to spot up-and-coming talent. Monthly rotating exhibitions keep the presentation fresh and pretty avant-garde.

❽ Tocaya Organica
Tocaya Organica (☎305-909-0799; www.tocayaorganica.com; 920 Lincoln Rd; ⏱11am-midnight Mon-Thu, to 2am Fri-Sun) whips up delicious modern Mexican fare with ample healthy and vegetarian options. The menu is a choose-your-own-adventure culinary style: pick from salads, tacos, burritos or veggie-based bowls, top with a protein (like mahi-mahi, veggie sausage or grilled steak) and cheese of choice, and enjoy.

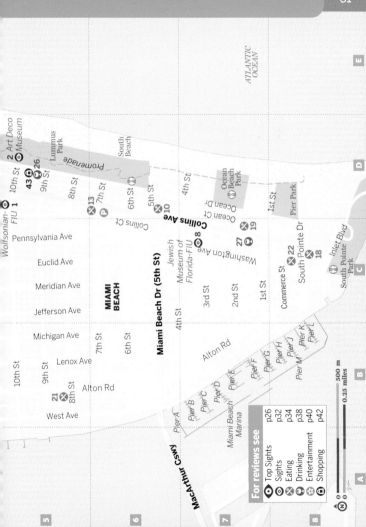

ATLANTIC OCEAN

Lummus Park

South Beach

Promenade

Ocean Beach Park

Pier Park

South Pointe Park

Wolfsonian-FIU 1

2 Art Deco Museum

10th St
9th St
8th St
7th St
6th St
5th St
4th St
1st St

43 26

13

10

8

19

27

22

18

Collins Ct

Collins Ave

Ocean Ct

Ocean Dr

Washington Ave

Jewish Museum of Florida-FIU

MIAMI BEACH

MIAMI BEACH DR (5th St)

Inlet Blvd

South Pointe Dr

Commerce St

1st St

2nd St

3rd St

4th St

6th St

7th St

Pennsylvania Ave

Euclid Ave

Meridian Ave

Jefferson Ave

Michigan Ave

Lenox Ave

West Ave

10th St

9th St

8th St

Alton Rd

21

Alton Rd

Pier A
Pier B
Pier C
Pier D
Pier E
Pier F
Pier G
Pier H
Pier J
Pier K
Pier L
Pier M

Miami Beach Marina

MacArthur Cswy

For reviews see	
◉ Top Sights	p26
◉ Sights	p32
⊗ Eating	p34
◯ Drinking	p38
◯ Entertainment	p40
◉ Shopping	p42

0   500 m
0   0.25 miles

Sights

Wolfsonian-FIU
MUSEUM

1 Map p30, D5

Visit this excellent design museum early in your stay to put the aesthetics of Miami Beach into context. It's one thing to see how wealth, leisure and the pursuit of beauty manifest in Miami Beach, but it's another to understand the roots and shadings of local artistic movements. By chronicling the interior evolution of everyday life, the Wolfsonian reveals how these trends manifested architecturally in SoBe's exterior deco. (☎305-531-1001; www.wolfsonian.org; 1001 Washington Ave; adult/child $10/5, 6-9pm Fri free; ⏱10am-6pm Mon, Tue, Thu & Sat, to 9pm Fri, noon-6pm Sun, closed Wed)

Art Deco Museum
MUSEUM

2 Map p30, D5

This small museum is one of the best places in town for an enlightening over-view of the art-deco district. Through videos, photography, models and other displays, you'll learn about the pioneering work of Barbara Capitman, who helped save these buildings from certain destruction back in the 1970s, and her collaboration with Leonard Horowitz, the talented artist who designed the pastel color palette that become an integral part of the design visible today. (www.mdpl.org/welcome-center/art-deco-museum; 1001 Ocean Dr; $5; ⏱10am-5pm Tue-Sun, to 7pm Thu)

South Beach
BEACH

3 Map p30, E4

When most people think of Miami Beach, they're envisioning South Beach, or 'SoBe.' This area is rife with clubs, bars, restaurants, models and a distinctive veneer of art-deco architecture. The beach itself en-compasses a lovely stretch of golden sands, dotted with colorful deco-style lifeguard stations. The shore gathers a wide mix of humanity, including suntanned locals and plenty of pale tourists, and gets crowded in high season (December to March) and on weekends when the weather is warm. (Ocean Dr; ⏱5am-midnight)

New World Center
NOTABLE BUILDING

4 Map p30, C2

Designed by Frank Gehry, this performance hall rises majestically out of a manicured lawn just above Lincoln Rd. Not unlike the ethereal power of the music within, the glass-and-steel facade encases charac-teristically Gehry-esque sail-like shapes within that help shape the magnificent acoustics and add to the futuristic quality of the concert hall. The grounds form a 2½-acre public park aptly known as **SoundScape Park** (www.nws.edu; 500 17th St). (☎305-673-3330, tours 305-673-3331; www.newworldcenter.com; 500 17th St; tours $5; ⏱tours 4pm Tue & Thu, 1pm Fri & Sat)

Jewish Museum of Florida-FIU (p34)

Holocaust Memorial

MEMORIAL

5 ⊙ Map p30, C1

Even for a Holocaust piece, this memorial is particularly powerful. With over 100 sculptures, its centerpiece is the Sculpture of Love and Anguish, an enormous, oxidized bronze arm with an artistic patina that bears an Auschwitz tattoo number – chosen because it was never issued at the camp, in order to represent all prisoners. Terrified families scale the sides of the arm, trying to pass their loved ones, including children, to safety only to see them later massacred, while below lie figures of all ages in various poses of suffering.

(www.holocaustmmb.org; cnr Meridian Ave & Dade Blvd; ⊙9:30am-10pm)

Española Way Promenade

AREA

6 ⊙ Map p30, D3

Española Way is an 'authentic' Spanish promenade...in the Florida theme-park spirit of authenticity. Oh, whatever; it's a lovely terracotta and cobbled arcade of rose-pink and Spanish-cream architecture, perfect for an alfresco meal, day or night, with a side of people-watching at one of the many restaurants lining the strip. (btwn 14th & 15th Sts)

The Bass
MUSEUM

7 ◉ Map p30, D1

The best art museum in Miami Beach has a playfully futuristic facade, a crisp interplay of lines and a bright, white-walled space – like an Orthodox church on a space-age Greek isle. All designed, by the way, in 1930 by Russell Pancoast (grandson of John A Collins, who lent his name to Collins Ave). The collection isn't shabby either: permanent highlights range from 16th-century European religious works to northern European and Renaissance paintings. (☑305-673-7530; www.thebass.org; 2121 Park Ave; adult/child $8/6; ⊙noon-5pm Wed & Thu, Sat & Sun, to 9pm Fri)

Jewish Museum of Florida-FIU
MUSEUM

8 ◉ Map p30, C7

Housed in a 1936 Orthodox synagogue that served Miami's first congregation, this small museum chronicles the rather large contribution Jews have made to the state of Florida. After all, it could be said that while Cubans made Miami, Jews made Miami Beach, both physically and culturally. Yet there were times when Jews were barred from the American Riviera they carved out of the sand, and this museum tells that story, along with some amusing anecdotes (like seashell Purim dresses). (☑305-672-5044; www.jmof.fiu.edu; 301 Washington Ave; adult/student & senior $6/5, Sat free; ⊙10am-5pm Tue-Sun, closed Jewish holidays)

World Erotic Art Museum
MUSEUM

9 ◉ Map p30, D4

In a neighborhood where no behavior is too shocking, the World Erotic Art Museum celebrates its staggering but artful pornography, including pieces by Rembrandt and Picasso. Back in 2005, 70-year-old Naomi Wilzig turned her 5000-piece erotica collection into a South Beach attraction. (☑305-532-9336; www.weam. com; 1205 Washington Ave; over 18yr $15; ⊙11am-10pm Mon-Thu, to midnight Fri-Sun)

Eating

Dirt
CAFE $

10 ✖ Map p30, D6

This stylish, sunlit cafe on busy 5th St draws a chatty cross-section of

Top Tip
Biking South Beach
One of the best ways to get around South Beach is by bicycle. The bike-sharing network Citi Bike has dozens of kiosks around, and checking out a bike is as easy as swiping a credit card, grabbing a bike and pedaling off. There's also a handy iPhone app (Citi Bike Miami) that shows nearby bike stations.

South Beach folk, who come for good coffee and deliciously healthy food options. Among the hits: roasted mushroom and raw-beet vegan wraps, white-bean hummus, and 'bowls' full of sautéed kale, chickpeas and other goodies. (www.dirteatclean.com; 232 5th St; mains $12-15; ⊙9am-9pm)

Taquiza
MEXICAN $

11 Map p30, D3

Taquiza has acquired a stellar reputation among Miami's street-food lovers. The take-out stand with a few outdoor tables serves up delicious perfection in its steak, pork, shrimp or veggie tacos (but no fish options) served on handmade blue-corn tortillas. They're small, so order a few. (305-748-6099; www.taquizamiami.com; 1506 Collins Ave; tacos $3.50-5; ⊙8am-midnight Sun-Thu, to 2am Fri & Sat)

La Sandwicherie
SANDWICHES $

12 Map p30, D3

Closed just a few hours each day, this boxcar long eatery does a roaring trade in filling baguette sandwiches sold at rock-bottom prices. Ingredients are fairly classic: roast beef, smoked salmon, avocado or combos like prosciutto with mozzarella, though you can load up with toppings for a deliciously satisfying meal. (305-532-8934; www.lasandwicherie.com; 229 14th St; mains $6-11; ⊙8am-5am Sun-Thu, to 6am Fri & Sat;)

Local Life
Secret Garden

The lush but little-known Miami Beach Botanical Garden (Map p30, B1) is small (just 2.6 acres) but feels like a veritable secret oasis in the midst of the urban jungle – encompassing palm trees, flowering hibiscus trees and glassy ponds. It's a great spot for a picnic.

Puerto Sagua
CUBAN $

13 Map p30, D6

There's a secret colony of older working-class Cubans and construction workers hidden among South Beach's sex-and-flash, and evidently they eat here. Puerto Sagua challenges the US diner with this reminder: Cubans can greasy-spoon with the best of them. Portions of favorites such as *picadillo* (spiced ground beef with rice, beans and plantains) are enormous. (305-673-1115; 700 Collins Ave; mains $8-18; ⊙7:30am-2am)

A La Folie
FRENCH $

14 Map p30, C3

It's easy to fall for this charming French cafe on the edge of picturesque Española Way. You can enjoy duck confit salad, a decadent onion soup and savory galettes (buckwheat crepes) before satisfying your sweet tooth with dessert crepes – try the Normande (with caramelized apples and Calvados cream sauce). (305-538-4484; www.alafoliecafe.com;

516 Española Way; mains $10-17; ⊙9am-midnight;)

Gelateria 4D ICE CREAM $

15 Map p30, C2

It's hot. You've been walking all day. You need ice cream, stat. Why hello, 4D! This is an excellent spot for creamy, pillowy waves of European-style frozen goodness, and based on the crowds it's the favorite ice cream on South Beach. (⊋305-538-5755; 670 Lincoln Rd; 2-/3-scoops $6/8; ⊙9am-midnight Sun-Thu, to 1:30am Fri & Sat)

Yardbird SOUTHERN US $$

16 Map p30, B2

Yardbird has earned a die-hard following for its delicious haute Southern comfort food. The kitchen churns out some nice shrimp and grits, St Louis–style pork ribs, charred okra, and biscuits with smoked brisket, but it's most famous for its supremely good plate of fried chicken, spiced watermelon and waffles with bourbon maple syrup. (⊋305-538-5220; www.runchickenrun.com/miami; 1600 Lenox Ave; mains $18-38; ⊙11am-midnight Mon-Fri, from 8:30am Sat & Sun;)

Pubbelly FUSION $$

17 Map p30, A1

Pubbelly's dining genre is hard to pinpoint, besides delicious. It skews between Asian, North American and Latin American, gleaning the best from all cuisines. Examples? Try black-truffle risotto, pork-belly dumplings or the mouthwatering kimchi fried rice with seafood. Hand-crafted cocktails wash down the dishes a treat. (⊋305-532-7555; www.pubbellyboys.com/miami/pubbelly; 1418 20th St; sharing plates $11-24, mains $19-30; ⊙6pm-midnight Tue-Thu & Sun, to 1am Fri & Sat;)

Lilikoi CAFE $$

18 Map p30, C8

Head to the quieter, southern end of South Beach for healthy, mostly organic and veg-friendly dishes at this laid-back, indoor-outdoor spot. Start the morning off with big bowls of açaí and granola or bagels with lox (and eggs Benedict on weekends); or linger over kale Caesar salads, mushroom risotto and falafel wraps at lunch. (⊋305-763-8692; www.lilikoiorganicliving.com; 500 S Pointe Dr; mains

○ Local Life
South Pointe Park

The very southern tip of Miami Beach has been converted into a lovely **park** (Map p31, 1C; ⊋305-673-7779; 1 Washington Ave; ⊙sunrise-10pm;), replete with manicured grass for lounging; a beach; views over a remarkably teal and fresh ocean; a restaurant; a refreshment stand; a tiny waterpark for kids; warm, scrubbed-stone walkways; and lots of folks who want to enjoy the great weather and views sans the South Beach strutting.

$12-20; ⏱8am-7pm Mon-Wed, to 8:30pm
Thu-Sun;)

Big Pink   DINER $$

19 Map p30, C7

Big Pink does American comfort
food with joie de vivre and a dash
of whimsy. The Americana menu is
consistently good throughout the
day; pulled Carolina pork holds the
table next to a nicely done Reuben.
The interior is somewhere between
a '50s sock hop and a South Beach
club; expect to be seated at a long
communal table. (☎305-532-4700; 157
Collins Ave; mains $13-26; ⏱8am-midnight
Sun-Wed, to 2am Thu, to 5am Fri & Sat)

Front Porch Cafe   AMERICAN $$

20 Map p30, D3

An open-sided perch just above the
madness of the cruising scene, the
Porch has been serving excellent
salads, sandwiches and the like since
1990 (eons by South Beach standards).
Breakfast is justifiably popular; the
challah French toast is delicious, as
are fluffy omelets, eggs Benedict and
strong coffees. (☎305-531-8300; www.
frontporchoceandrive.com; 1458 Ocean Dr;
mains $10-25; ⏱7am-11pm;)

Macchialina   ITALIAN $$$

21 Map p30, B5

This buzzing Italian trattoria has all
the right ingredients for a terrific
night out; namely great service and
beautifully turned-out cooking,

Joe's Stone Crab Restaurant

served in a warm rustic-chic interior
of exposed brick and chunky wood
tables (plus outdoor tables in front).
(☎305-534-2124; www.macchialina.com;
820 Alton Rd; mains $23-32)

Joe's Stone
Crab Restaurant   AMERICAN $$$

22 Map p30, C8

The wait is long and the prices for
iconic dishes can be high. But if
those aren't deal-breakers, queue up
to don a bib in Miami's most famous
restaurant (around since 1913!) and
enjoy deliciously fresh-stone crab
claws. (☎305-673-0365; www.joesstone
crab.com; 11 Washington Ave; mains lunch

Local Life
Outdoor Screenings

From October through May, SoundsScape Park (p32; Map p30, D1) has weekly film screenings (currently Wednesdays at 8pm) – usually cult classics. Located outside of the New World Center, a 7000-sq-ft projection plays on the Frank Gehry–designed concert hall. In addition, some performances happening inside the hall are projected simultaneously outside. Bring a picnic and enjoy the show.

$14-30, dinner $19-60; ⏱11:30am-2:30pm Tue-Sat, 5-10pm daily)

Yuca   LATIN AMERICAN $$$

23 🍴 Map p30, C2

This was one of the first Nuevo Latino hot spots in Miami and it's still going strong. The elegant candelit dining room sets the stage for lingering over plates of shrimp enchiladas, tender guava ribs and tuna tatake salad made of seared tuna, mango and sweet chili dressing. (☎305-532-9822; www.yuca.com; 501 Lincoln Rd; mains $24-52, sharing plates $9-24; ⏱noon-11pm Sun-Thu, to midnight Fri & Sat)

Drinking

Sweet Liberty   BAR

24 🍷 Map p30, D1

A much-loved local haunt near Collins Park, Sweet Liberty has all the right ingredients for a fun night out: friendly, easygoing bartenders who whip up excellent cocktails (try a mint julep), great happy-hour specials (including 75¢ oysters) and a relaxed, pretension-free crowd. The space is huge, with flickering candles, a long wooden bar and the odd band adding to the cheer. (www.mysweetliberty.com; 237 20th St; ⏱4pm-5am Mon-Sat, from noon Sun)

Bodega   COCKTAIL BAR

25 🍷 Map p30, B3

Bodega looks like your average hipster Mexican joint – serving up delicious tacos ($3 to $5) from a converted Airstream trailer to a party-minded crowd. But there's actually a bar hidden behind that blue porta-potty door on the right. Head inside (or join the long line on weekends) to take in a bit of old-school glam in a sprawling drinking den. (☎305-704-2145; www.bodegasouthbeach.com; 1220 16th St; ⏱noon-5am)

Mango's Tropical Café   BAR

26 🍷 Map p30, D5

A mix of Latin-loving locals and visitors from far-flung corners of the globe mix things up at this famous bar on Ocean Dr. Every night feels like a celebration, with a riotously fun vibe, and plenty of entertainment: namely minimally dressed staff dancing on the bar, doing Michael Jackson impersonations, shimmying in feather headdresses or showing off some amazing salsa

moves. (📞305-673-4422; www.man-
gostropicalcafe.com; 900 Ocean Dr; $10;
🕙11:45am-5am)

Story
CLUB

27 Map p30, C7

For the big megaclub experience, Story
is a top destination. Some of the best
DJs (mostly EDM) from around the
globe spin at this club, with parties
lasting late into the night. It has a fairly
roomy dance floor, but gets packed on
weekend nights. Be good looking and
dress to impress, as getting in can be
a pain. (📞305-479-4426; www.storymiami.
com; 136 Collins Ave; 🕙11pm-5am Thu-Sun)

Bay Club
COCKTAIL BAR

28 Map p30, A1

A great little nightspot in Sunset
Harbour, Bay Club has an enticing low-
lit vintage vibe with red banquettes,
antique wallpaper, wood paneling and
old chandeliers. It's a good date spot
with craft cocktails and occasional live
music (jazz guitar and other subdued
sounds). (📞305-695-4441; 1930 Bay Rd;
🕙5pm-2am)

Campton Yard
BEER GARDEN

29 Map p30, D3

Spread beneath a towering banyan
tree, this pebble-strewn backyard
draws a youthful crowd who come
for a night of laid-back merriment
beneath the faerie lights. There are
games (giant Jenga and Connect 4,
ping pong, beanbag tossing), craft

beer, picnic tables and a welcome
lack of pretension. Enter through the
Hall Hotel, and make your way to the
backyard oasis. (1500 Collins Ave, Hall
Hotel; 🕙5pm-midnight Mon-Fri, from noon
Sat & Sun)

Kill Your Idol
BAR

30 Map p30, D3

Kill Your Idol is a bit of a dive, but it
has plenty of appeal, with graffiti and
shelves full of retro bric-a-brac covering the walls, drag shows on Monday
and DJs spinning danceable old-school
grooves. The crowd is a fairly laid-back
mix of locals and out-of-towners. The
bar is tiny, so prepare for the crowds
on weekends. (📞305-672-1852; www.killy
ouridol.com; 222 Española Way; 🕙8pm-5am)

Rose Bar at the Delano
BAR

31 Map p30, D2

The ultrachic Rose Bar at this
elegant Ian Schrager original is a

☑️ Top Tip

Escaping the Crowds

Ocean Dr can feel a bit cheesy.
Expect high prices and a circus-
like feel to the dining or drinking
experience if you take a seat here.
To escape the mayhem, head to
Sunset Harbour or SoFi (south
of Fifth), where you'll find a more
local crowd, and generally much
higher quality when it comes to
food and drink.

watering hole for beautiful creatures (or at least those with a healthy ego). Get ready to pay up for the privilege – but also prepare to enjoy it. (🗷305-674-5752; www.delano-hotel.com; 1685 Collins Ave, Delano Hotel; ⏰noon-2am)

Mynt
CLUB

32 🚇 Map p30, D1

Join the partying stars – Justin Timberlake, Vin Diesel, Britney Spears, Real Housewives, etc – by bottle servicing yourself into the VIP section. Otherwise, make friends with the red rope until you can order a drink and then try not to spill it, which is tough in the sweaty scrum of models, Moët and mojitos. (🗷305-532-0727; www.mynt lounge.com; 1921 Collins Ave; ⏰11:30pm-5am Fri & Sat)

Abbey Brewery
MICROBREWERY

33 🚇 Map p30, B2

The oldest brew-pub in South Beach is on the untouristed end of South Beach (near Alton Rd). It's friendly and packed with folks listening to throwback hits (grunge, '80s new wave) and slinging back some excellent homebrew: give Father Theo's stout or the Immaculate IPA a try. (www.abbeybrewing inc.com; 1115 16th St; ⏰1pm-5am)

Twist
GAY

34 🚇 Map p30, D4

Never a cover, always a groove, this two-story gay club has some serious

staying power and a little bit of something for everyone: six different bars; go-go dancers; drag shows; lounging areas and a small dance floor. (🗷305-538-9478; www.twistsobe. com; 1057 Washington Ave; ⏰1pm-5am)

Lost Weekend
BAR

35 🚇 Map p30, D3

The Weekend is a grimy, sweaty, slovenly dive, filled with pool tables, cheap domestics and – hell yeah – *Golden Tee* and *Big Buck Hunter* arcade games. God bless it. Popular with local waiters, kitchen staff and bartenders. (🗷305-672-1707; www. sub-culture.org/lost-weekend-miami; 218 Española Way; ⏰noon-5am)

Entertainment

New World Symphony
CLASSICAL MUSIC

36 ⭐ Map p30, C2

Housed in the New World Center (p32) – a funky explosion of cubist lines and geometric curves, fresh white against the blue Miami sky – the acclaimed New World Symphony holds performances from October to May. The deservedly heralded NWS serves as a three- to four-year preparatory program for talented musicians from prestigious music schools. (NWS; 🗷305-673-3330; www. nws.edu; 500 17th St)

Colony Theater

Colony Theater

PERFORMING ARTS

37 Map p30, B2

The Colony is an absolute art-deco gem, with a classic marquee and Inca-style crenellations, which looks like the sort of place gangsters would go to watch *Hamlet*. This treasure now serves as a major venue for performing arts – from comedy and occasional musicals to theatrical dramas, off-Broadway productions and ballet – as well as hosting movie screenings and small film festivals. (☏305-674-1040, box office 800-211-1414; www.colonymb.org; 1040 Lincoln Rd)

Fillmore Miami Beach

PERFORMING ARTS

38 Map p30, C1

Built in 1951, South Beach's premier showcase for touring Broadway shows, orchestras and other big musical productions has 2700 seats and excellent acoustics. Jackie Gleason chose to make the theater his home for the long-running 1960s TV show, but now you'll find an eclectic lineup: Catalan pop or indie rock one night, the comedian Bill Maher or an over-the-top vaudeville group the next. (☏305-673-7300; www.fillmoremb.com; 1700 Washington Ave)

Shopping

Books & Books

BOOKS

39 🔒 Map p30, B2

Stop in this fantastic indie bookstore for an excellent selection of new fiction, beautiful art and photography books, award-winning children's titles and more. The layout – a series of elegantly furnished rooms – invites endless browsing, and there's a good restaurant and cafe in front of the store. (📞305-532-3222; www.booksandbooks.com; 927 Lincoln Rd; ⏱10am-11pm Sun-Thu, to midnight Fri & Sat)

Havaianas

FASHION & ACCESSORIES

40 🔒 Map p30, C2

The well-known Brazilian flip-flop (thong) brand serves up lots of different colors and styles (with plenty of recognizable Disney characters for the kids) at their popular shop on Lincoln Rd. You can also add custom embellishments: tiny hearts, diamonds, rhinestones and fleur de lys placed on the strap. (https://us.havaianas.com; 831 Lincoln Rd; ⏱10am-10pm Mon-Sat, 11am-9pm Sun)

Nomad Tribe

CLOTHING

41 🔒 Map p30, D3

Like the flagship store in Wynwood (p86), Nomad Tribe focuses on fair-trade products and ethically produced items – which aren't short on style. Intriguing bracelets by indie designers and eye-catching clothing and vegan footwear are all part of the draw.

(www.nomadtribeshop.com; 1510 Washington Ave; ⏱noon-9pm)

Base

CLOTHING

42 🔒 Map p30, B2

This attractive shop, carrying mostly men's wear, on Lincoln Rd has lots of stylish gear for a wardrobe update. Herschel bags, high-tech outerwear by Nanamica, finely crafted jeans by Neuw Denim, chunky brass bracelets and Mykita sunglasses are among the one-of-a-kind brands on hand. (📞305-531-4982; www.baseworld.com; 939 Lincoln Rd; ⏱11am-10pm)

U Rock Couture

CLOTHING

43 🔒 Map p30, D5

U Rock is the quintessential South Beach clothing store. Loud, flashy and in your face, it resembles a mangled clash of rhinestones, tight clothes, revealing dresses, deep tans, euro accents and the cast of *Jersey Shore*. Somehow, this is all strangely appealing...rather like certain pockets of South Beach. (📞877-805-2422; www.urockcouture.com; 928 Ocean Dr; ⏱10am-1am)

Ricky's NYC

GIFTS & SOUVENIRS

44 🔒 Map p30, C2

This South Beach standby boasts hundreds of tacky gifts (boxing-nun puppets), pop-art paraphernalia and, well, 'adult' accoutrements of sex toys, games, costumes and other unmentionables. (📞305-674-8511; www.rickysnyc.com; 536 Lincoln Rd; ⏱10am-midnight)

Understand

Rise of a Beachside City

It's always been the weather that's attracted Miami's two most prominent species: developers and tourists. But it wasn't the sun per se that got people moving here – it was an ice storm. The great Florida freeze of 1895 wiped out the state's citrus industry; at the same time, widowed Julia Tuttle bought out parcels of land that would become modern Miami, and Henry Flagler was building his Florida East Coast Railroad. Tuttle offered to split her land with Flagler if he extended the railway to Miami, but the train man didn't pay her any heed until north Florida froze over and Tuttle sent him an 'I told you so' message: an orange blossom clipped from her Miami garden.

The rest is a history of boom, bust, dreamers and opportunists. Generally, Miami has grown in leaps and bounds following major world events and natural disasters. Hurricanes (particularly the deadly Great Miami Hurricane of 1926) have wiped away the town, but it just keeps bouncing back and building better than before.

20th-Century Growth

Miami Beach blossomed in the early 20th century when Jewish developers recognized the potential American Riviera in their midst. Those hoteliers started building resorts that were branded with a distinctive art-deco facade by daring architects willing to buck the more staid aesthetics of the northeast. The world wars brought soldiers who were stationed at nearby naval facilities, many of whom liked the sun and decided to stay. Latin American and Caribbean revolutions introduced immigrants from the other direction, most famously from Cuba. Cuban immigrants arrived in two waves: first, the anti-Castro types of the '60s, and those looking for a better life since the late 1970s, such as the arrivals on the 1980 Mariel Boatlift during a Cuban economic crisis. The glam and overconsumption of the 1980s, as shown in movies such as *Scarface* and *Miami Beach*, attracted a certain breed of the rich and beautiful, and their associated models, designers, hoteliers and socialites, all of whom transformed South Beach into the beautiful beast it is today.

Explore

Northern Miami Beach

The long condo-studded landscape of North Beach offers a slightly different version of Miami Beach decadence. Here instead of art deco, you'll find the so-called MiMo (Miami Modernist) style of grand buildings constructed in the post-WWII boom days. Although there are fewer restaurants, bars and shops, North Beach has plenty of allure, starting with its gorgeous beachfront.

The Sights in a Day

☀ Begin the day with a walk along the verdant **Boardwalk** (p48), followed by a peaceful crowd-free stroll on the beach. Afterwards check out some of the neighborhood's monumental architecture in the likes of **Fontainebleau** (pictured left; p47) and **Eden Roc Renaissance** (p47).

☼ Have a seafood lunch at **Fifi's Place** (p50), then head up to **Oleta River State Park** (p48) for a bit of adventure in the great outdoors. Hire kayaks for a peaceful paddle in the Oleta River Estuary and look for wildlife on the nature trails. In the late afternoon, treat yourself to a spa treatment at the **Carillon Miami Wellness Resort** (p47). Or for something decidedly less bourgeois, beat yourself with a birch branch in the steamy **Russian & Turkish Baths** (p48).

☾ In the evening, book a table at **27 Restaurant** (p49) for creative Modern American cooking in a buzzing, very hip setting. Afterwards, stick around for creative cocktails in the lush adjoining courtyard of **Broken Shaker** (p50). If you're still going strong late in the night, head over to **Liv** (p50), for a dance party with the beautiful crowd.

 Best of Miami

Eating
27 Restaurant (p49)

Cafe Prima Pasta (p49)

Josh's Deli (p49)

Drinking & Nightlife
Broken Shaker (p50)

Sandbar Lounge (p50)

WunderBar (p51)

Getting There

🚌 **Bus** Several buses, including routes 119 and 120, go along Collins Ave, connecting South Beach and points north.

🚲 **Bike** There are many Citi Bike stations along this stretch of Miami Beach, found as far north as 103rd St and Bay Harbor Dr.

🚗 **Car** Finding parking is easier than down in South Beach, but it can still be challenging.

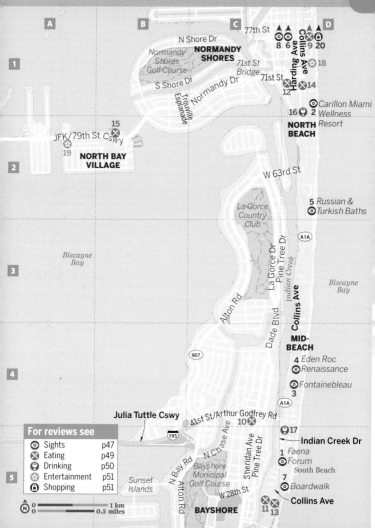

A | **B** | **C** | **D**

77th St

Collins Ave

N Shore Dr

**NORMANDY
SHORES**

Harding Ave

8 6

9 20

*Normandy
Shores
Golf Course*

71st St
Bridge

71st St

18

S Shore Dr

Normandy Dr

12

14

Trouville
Esplanade

16 2

Carillon Miami
Wellness
Resort

15

**NORTH
BEACH**

JFK/79th St Cswy

19

**NORTH BAY
VILLAGE**

W 63rd St

*Biscayne
Bay*

*La Gorce
Country
Club*

5 Russian &
Turkish Baths

A1A

La Gorce Dr
Pine Tree Dr

Indian Creek

*Biscayne
Bay*

Alton Rd

Dade Blvd

Collins Ave

**MID-
BEACH**

907

4 Eden Roc
Renaissance

3 Fontainebleau

A1A

Julia Tuttle Cswy

41st St/Arthur Godfrey Rd

10

17

195

N Chase Ave

Indian Creek Dr

1 Faena
Forum

Sheridan Ave
Pine Tree Dr

*Bayshore
Municipal
Golf Course*

South Beach

7 Boardwalk

*Sunset
Islands*

N Bay Rd

Alton Rd

W 28th St

Collins Ave

11 13

BAYSHORE

N

0 ——— 1 km
0 ——— 0.5 miles

Sights

Faena Forum
CULTURAL CENTER

1 Map p46, D5

Part of the ambitious new $1 billion Faena District, this new cultural center has been turning heads ever since its opening in late 2016. The circular Rem Koolhaas–designed building features rooms for performances, exhibitions, lectures and other events. Check the website to see what's coming up. (www.faena.com; Collins Ave & 33rd St)

Carillon Miami Wellness Resort
SPA

2 Map p46, D1

For pure pampering, the Carillon's 70,000-sq-ft spa and wellness center is hard to knock. It has an excellent range of treatments and fitness classes (spinning, power yoga, meditation, core workouts) plus pretty views of the crashing waves. (☏866-276-2226; www.carillonhotel.com; 6801 Collins Ave, Carillon Hotel; treatments $165-300; ⏰8am-9pm)

Fontainebleau
HISTORIC BUILDING

3 Map p46, D4

As you proceed north on Collins, the condos and apartment buildings grow in grandeur and embellishment until you enter an area nicknamed Millionaire's Row. The most fantastic jewel in this glittering crown is the **Fontainebleau hotel** (☏305-535-3283; www.fontainebleau.com; 4441 Collins Ave). The hotel – mainly the pool, which

Oleta River State Park (p48)

has since been renovated – features in Brian de Palma's classic *Scarface*.

Eden Roc Renaissance
HISTORIC BUILDING

4 Map p46, D4

The Eden Roc was the second groundbreaking resort from Morris Lapidus, and it's a fine example of the architecture known as MiMo (Miami Modern). It was the hangout for the 1960s Rat Pack – Sammy Davis Jr, Dean Martin, Frank Sinatra and crew. Extensive renovation has eclipsed some of Lapidus' style, but with that said, the building is still an iconic piece of Miami Beach architecture, and an exemplar of the brash beauty of Millionaire's Row. (www.nobuedenroc.com; 4525 Collins Ave)

Top Tip

Greeting the Day

Don't miss a sunrise walk along the pretty beachfront. Early morning is a peaceful time, with few people on the sands, and the chance to have those golden, sometimes rose-tinted views to yourself. The light can also be pure magic when photographing those iconic lifeguard stations.

Russian & Turkish Baths

MASSAGE

5 ◉ Map p46, D2

Just because you enjoy a good back rub doesn't mean you need to go to some glitzy spa where they constantly play soft house music on a repetitive loop. Right? Why not head to a favorite 'hot' spot among folks who want a spa experience without the glamour. Enter this little labyrinth of *banyas* (steam rooms) for a plethora of spa choices. (☎305-867-8316; www.russianandturkishbaths.com; 5445 Collins Ave; treatments from $40; ⊙noon-midnight)

Oleta River State Park

STATE PARK

6 ◉ Map p46, D1

Tequesta people were boating the Oleta River estuary as early as 500 BC, so you're just following in a long tradition if you canoe or kayak in this park. At almost 1000 acres, this is the largest urban park in the state and one of the best places in Miami to escape the madding crowd. Boat out to the local mangrove island, watch the eagles fly by, or just chill on the pretension-free beach. (☎305-919-1844; www.floridastateparks.org/oletariver; 3400 NE 163rd St; vehicle/pedestrian & bicycle $6/2; ⊙8am-sunset; P 👪)

Boardwalk

BEACH

7 ◉ Map p46, D5

What's trendy in beachwear this season? Seventeenth-century Polish gabardine coats, apparently. There are plenty of skimpily dressed hotties on the Mid-Beach boardwalk, but there are also Orthodox Jews going about their business in the midst of joggers, strolling tourists and sunbathers. Nearby are numerous condo buildings occupied by middle-class Latinos and Jews, who walk their dogs and play with their kids here, giving the entire place a laid-back, real-world vibe that contrasts with the nonstop glamour of South Beach. (www.miamibeachboardwalk.com; 21st St-46th St)

Haulover Beach Park

PARK

8 ◉ Map p46, C1

Where are all those tanned men in gold chains and Speedos going? That would be the clothing-optional beach in this 40-acre park hidden from condos, highways and prying eyes by vegetation. There's more to do here than get in the buff, though; most of the beach is 'normal' (there's even a dog park) and is one of the nicer spots for sand in the area. The park is on Collins Ave about 4.5 miles north of 71st St.

(305-947-3525; www.miamidade.gov/parks/
haulover.asp; 10800 Collins Ave; per car Mon-
Fri $5, Sat-Sun $7; ⊙sunrise-sunset; P)

Eating

Josh's Deli   DELI $

9 ✖ Map p46, D1

Josh's is simplicity itself. Here in the
heart of Jewish Miami, you can nosh
on thick cuts of house-cured pastrami
sandwiches and matzo-ball soup for
lunch or challah French toast, eggs and
house-cured salmon for breakfast. It's a
deliciously authentic slice of Mid-Beach
culture. (305-397-8494; www.joshsdeli.
com; 9517 Harding Ave; sandwiches $14-16;
⊙8:30am-3:30pm)

Roasters 'n Toasters   DELI $

10 ✖ Map p46, C4

Given the crowds and the satisfied
smiles of customers, Roasters 'n Toast-
ers meets the demanding standards of
Miami Beach's large Jewish demographic, thanks to juicy deli meat, fresh
bread, crispy bagels and warm latkes.
Sliders (mini-sandwiches) are served
on challah bread, an innovation that's
as charming as it is tasty. (305-531-
7691; www.roastersntoasters.com; 525 Arthur
Godfrey Rd; mains $10-18; ⊙6:30am-3:30pm)

27 Restaurant   FUSION $$

11 ✖ Map p46, C5

This new spot sits on the grounds of
the very popular Broken Shaker (p50),
one of Miami Beach's best-loved
cocktail bars. Like the bar, the setting
is amazing – akin to dining in an
old tropical cottage, with worn wood
floorboards, candlelit tables, and
various rooms slung with artwork and
curious knickknacks, plus a lovely terrace. The cooking is exceptional, and
incorporates flavors from around the
globe. (786-476-7020; www.freehand
hotels.com/miami/27-restaurant; 2727 Indian
Creek Dr; mains $17-28; ⊙6:30pm-2am Mon-
Sat, 11am-4pm & 6:30pm-2am Sun; ✖)

Cafe Prima Pasta   ITALIAN $$

12 ✖ Map p46, D1

We're not sure what's better at this
Argentine-Italian place: the much-
touted pasta, which deserves every one
of the accolades heaped on it, or the
atmosphere, which captures the digni-
fied sultriness of Buenos Aires. You
can't go wrong with the small, well-
curated menu, with standouts including gnocchi formaggi, baked branzino,
and squid-ink linguine with seafood in
a lobster sauce. (305-867-0106; www.
cafeprimapasta.com; 414 71st St; mains $17-
26; ⊙5-11:30pm Mon-Sat, 4-11pm Sun)

Indomania   INDONESIAN $$

13 ✖ Map p46, C5

There's a lot of watered-down Asian
cuisine in Miami; Indomania bucks
this trend with an authentic execution
of dishes from Southeast Asia's largest
nation. Dishes reflect Indonesia's diver-
sity, ranging from braised beef in spicy
coconut sauce to gut-busting *rijsttafel*,

a sort of buffet of small, tapas-style dishes that reflects the culinary character of particular Indonesian regions. (📞305-535-6332; www.indomaniarestaurant.com; 131 26th St; mains $18-32; ⏲5:30-10:30pm Mon-Sun, plus noon-4pm Sat & Sun)

Fifi's Place   SEAFOOD $$

14 🍴 Map p46, D1

Latin seafood is the name of the game here – Fifi's does delicious seafood paella, a dish that mixes the supporting cast of *The Little Mermaid* with Spanish rice, and an equally good seafood *parrillada*, which draws on the same ingredients and grills them with garlic butter. Outstanding. (📞305-865-5665; www.fifisseafood.com; 6934 Collins Ave; mains $16-32; ⏲noon-11pm)

Shuckers   AMERICAN $$

15 🍴 Map p46, B2

With excellent views overlooking the waters from the 79th St Causeway, Shuckers has to be one of the best-positioned restaurants around. The food is pub grub: burgers, fried fish and the like. The chicken wings, basted in several mouthwatering sauces, deep-fried and grilled again, are famous. (📞305-866-1570; www.shuckersbarandgrill.com; 1819 79th St Causeway; mains $12-27; ⏲11am-1am; 📶)

Drinking

Broken Shaker   BAR

Craft cocktails are having their moment in Miami, and if mixology is in the spotlight, you can bet Broken Shaker (see 11 🍴 Map p46, C5;) is sharing the glare. Expert bartenders run this spot, located in the back of the **Freehand Miami hotel** (www.thefreehand.com), which takes up one closet-sized indoor niche and a sprawling plant-filled courtyard of excellent drinks and beautiful people. (📞305-531-2727; www.freehandhotels.com/miami/broken-shaker; 2727 Indian Creek Dr, Freehand Miami Hotel; ⏲6pm-3am Mon-Fri, 2pm-3am Sat & Sun)

Sandbar Lounge   BAR

16 🍸 Map p46, D1

True to its name this dive bar has sand – lots and lots of it covering the floor. Never mind that the beach is a block away, Sandbar's a local institution, and a fine antidote to the high-end drinking spots covering Miami Beach. It has a welcoming vibe, sports on TV, a fun jukebox and great happy-hour specials. Come on in and join the gang. (📞305-865-1752; 6752 Collins Ave; ⏲4pm-5am)

Liv   CLUB

The top nightspot in Miami Beach for the glitterati is an 18,000-sq-ft hall of decadence lavishly set inside the Fontainebleau Hotel (see 3 ⚪ Map p46, D4); a celebrity magnet in its own right. Getting in, however, is a nightmare if you're not wealthy (men) or extremely good looking (women). By all means, go if you have a connection, otherwise, it's not worth the hassle. (📞305-674-4680; www.livnightclub.com; 4441 Collins Ave, Fontainebleau Hotel)

WunderBar LOUNGE

17 🚇 Map p46, D5

Tucked off to the back of **Circa 39's** (☎305-538-4900) moody front lobby, this designer dream bar has a warm, welcoming feel to it. Definitely stop in for a drink if you're up this way, before sauntering across the street and checking out the lapping waves on the beach. (☎305-503-1120; www.circa39.com/wunderbar; 3900 Collins Ave, Circa39; ⏰11am-11pm Sun-Thu, to midnight Fri & Sat)

Entertainment

North Beach Bandshell LIVE MUSIC

18 ⭐ Map p46, D1

This outdoor venue features an excellent lineup of concerts, dance, theater, opera and spoken word throughout the year. Some events are free. It's run by the nonprofit Rhythm Foundation, and the wide-ranging repertoire features sounds from around the globe, with many family-friendly events. Check online to see what's on the roster. (www.northbeachbandshell.com; 7275 Collins Ave)

Chopin Foundation of the United States CLASSICAL MUSIC

19 ⭐ Map p46, A2

This national organization hosts a treasure trove of performances for Chopin fans – the Chopin Festival, a series of free monthly concerts and the less-frequent National Chopin Piano Competition, an international contest held in Miami every five years. (☎305-868-0624; www.chopin.org; 1440 JFK/79th St Causeway)

Shopping

Bal Harbour Shops MALL

20 🔒 Map p46, D1

A classy scene boasting Prada, Gucci, Chanel and Saks Fifth Avenue outposts. Bal Harbour is located about 3 miles north of North Miami Beach. (www.balharbourshops.com; 9700 Collins Ave; ⏰10am-9pm Mon-Sat, noon-6pm Sun)

⭕ Local Life
Keeping It Kosher in Miami Beach

They're no shtetls, but Arthur Godfrey Rd (41st St) and Harding Ave between 91st and 96th Sts in Surfside are popular thoroughfares for the Jewish population of Miami Beach. Just as Jews have shaped Miami Beach, so has the beach shaped its Jewish community: you can eat *lox y arroz con moros* (salmon with rice and beans); the Orthodox men don yarmulkes and the women wear head-scarves, and many have nice tans and drive flashy SUVs.

Explore

Downtown Miami

Downtown Miami, the city's international financial and banking center, is split between tatty indoor shopping arcades and new condos and high-rise luxury hotels in the area known as Brickell. The lazy, gritty Miami River divides Downtown into north and south. Miami is defined by an often frenetic pace of growth, with construction a near constant as new luxury towers arrive with each passing month.

The Sights in a Day

☀ Start the day with a delicious breakfast and outstanding coffee at **All Day** (p66). Once fortified, make your way to the **Pérez Art Museum Miami** (p54) for a look at some of the city's top art exhibitions. Be sure to take in the views and outdoor sculptures from the grounds.

☀ Around lunchtime, book a table at **Casablanca** (p66), a seafood-loving emporium with tables peacefully set alongside the Miami River. Following lunch, delve into Miami's past at **HistoryMiami** (p64), which gives a fascinating overview of the jumble of cultures and events that helped shape the city of today. After taking it all in, take a waterside break at **Bayfront Park** (p58), Downtown Miami's best-loved green space.

☾ In the evening, have an early dinner of delectable Peruvian fare at **CVI.CHE 105** (p68). Afterwards, catch a show at the stunning **Adrienne Arsht Center for the Performing Arts** (p56). End the night with drinks and a view at one of Miami's rooftop bars. **Sugar** (p61) offers a magnificent panorama of the city skyline from its 40th-floor perch.

For a local's day in Downtown Miami, see p60.

◉ Top Sights

Pérez Art Museum Miami (p54)

Adrienne Arsht Center for the Performing Arts (p56)

Bayfront Park (p58)

◯ Local Life

Downtown & Brickell (p60)

♥ Best of Miami

Eating
Casablanca (p66)

Verde (p67)

Drinking & Nightlife
Blackbird Ordinary (p68)

Sugar (p61)

Shopping
Supply & Advise (p61)

Mary Brickell Village (p71)

Getting There

Ⓜ **Metromover** A handy free downtown monorail

🚋 **Bus** The free Biscayne trolley gets you up north via Biscayne Blvd to the edge of Wynwood at 29th St. and the Design District at 39th St.

⚓ **Boat** Water Taxi Miami provides ferry transport between South Beach and the Bayside Marketplace in Downtown Miami.

Top Sights
Pérez Art Museum Miami

Miami has no shortage of first-rate galleries and intriguing museums. The Pérez, though, is in a category of its own. This gorgeous building, designed by a Pritzker Prize–winning architecture firm, houses a world-class collection of contemporary art – which is all the more impressive when viewed in its light-filled galleries on the edge of Biscayne Bay.

👁 Map p62, E1

www.pamm.org

1103 Biscayne Blvd

adult/seniors & students $16/12, 1st Thu & 2nd Sat of month free

🕙10am-6pm Fri-Tue, to 9pm Thu, closed Wed

The Architecture

Swiss architects Herzog & de Meuron designed this 200,000-sq-ft space, which opened to much fanfare in 2013. The three-story building sits on an elevated platform that gives it fine views over the water and the grassy park abutting it.

One of the most striking features of the building is its hanging gardens, the long columnlike tubes dangling from the rooftop. Each one is bursting with plants. In fact, there are more than 77 plant species – all native to the region – that are nourished by rainwater fed through cleverly concealed irrigation tubes within the columns.

The Art

PAMM stages some of the best contemporary exhibitions in Miami. The permanent collection rotates through unique pieces every few months (even as new artworks are acquired throughout the year). These are typically on the ground floor, and might explore a wide variety of themes – from the idea of geography's role in shaping perception to ideology and the intersection of advertising, commerce and politics. These galleries pull from a treasure trove of work spanning the last 80 years, which is assembled in exhibitions that are always thought-provoking and at times powerful.

Social Spaces

The designers of the museum wanted to create a place that all Miami residents feel they have access to. And in many ways, they succeeded remarkably. You can come and hang out in the grassy park, or sit on the steps or the deck chairs enjoying the views over the water. Then there is the restaurant, which feels less like a staid museum eatery, and more like a cafe with outdoor seating that happens to be next to a great collection of art.

☑ Top Tips

▶ Take advantage of free admission days. PAMM is free on the first Thursday and the second Saturday of the month.

▶ Museum guides lead excellent free 45-minute tours daily (except Wednesday) at 11am, noon and 2:30pm, as well as 6:30pm Thursday.

▶ Check the online calendar for upcoming film screenings, gallery talks and art-making workshops.

✗ Take a Break

Stop by Verde (p67) for salads, sandwiches, drinks and fine views. Outside the museum, Books & Books (p71) has a lovely cafe with outdoor seating.

Top Sights
Adrienne Arsht Center for the Performing Arts

New York has the Lincoln Center, Sydney has its Opera House, and Miami has the Adrienne Arsht Center, a much-loved performing arts hall, where you can see some of the world's top ballets, musical soloists and theatrical productions.

Map p62, D1

305-949-6722

www.arshtcenter.org

1300 Biscayne Blvd

box office 10am-6pm Mon-Fri, and 2 hr before performances

Three Venues in One

The first thing to know is that the Arsht Center comprises three separate venues. The biggest hall is found in the Ziff Ballet Opera House. This 2400-seat venue stages ballets, musicals, Broadway shows and, of course, opera.

Across Biscayne Blvd – and reachable by a pedestrian ramp – is the Knight Concert Hall. This 2200-seat, three-tiered theater is for musical concerts, and has some of the world's best acoustics.

The smallest venue is the 300-seat Carnival Studio Theater, a flexible black-box space that's located inside the Ziff Ballet Opera House.

The Design

The Arsht Center was designed by the firm of César Pelli, and there are some extraordinary features to the concert halls.

Artful touches are spread throughout. José Bedia designed the etched-glass railings visible in the upper tiers of the two concert halls. In one unbroken handstroke he drew musical instruments, fish, birds, palm trees, even cruise ships – symbols that blend the arts with the Miami landscape.

The Location

On the 2nd and 3rd floors of the Ziff Ballet Opera House, you can gaze through the floor-to-ceiling windows out over the landscape of Downtown Miami. It's a remarkable vantage point, and all the more striking given that so many of the skyscrapers on view weren't here a decade or so ago.

On Stage

The center stages a staggering number of performances each year – around 300 in fact. These are divided into various series, such as the Masterworks Season, Broadway in Miami, Jazz Roots and the Miami Made Festival, among other offerings.

JOHNNY LOUIS/FILMMAGIC/GETTY IMAGES ©

Top Sights
Bayfront Park

Folks from all walks of life flock to this green oasis on the edge of Downtown Miami. Aside from marvelous views over the water, this is the place for leisurely strolls, picnics on the grass, open-air concerts, free yoga sessions and even high-flying trapeze classes.

◉ Map p62, E5

☎ 305-358-7550

www.bayfrontparkmiami.com

301 N Biscayne Blvd

Concerts & Big Events in the Park

Throughout the year, Bayfront Park hosts a mix of big and small events, including the **Ultra Music Festival** (www.ultramusicfestival.com), which takes over the entire park for three days in late March. It also hosts one of South Florida's best fireworks shows, the Independence Day pyrotechnics that fill the night sky on July 4th.

Noguchi Sculptures

Renowned artist and landscape architect Isamu Noguchi redesigned much of the 32-acre Bayfront Park in the 1980s, and in so doing helped to revitalize Miami's barren Downtown.

In addition to the design, Noguchi dotted the grounds with three of his own sculptures. The Light Tower is a 40ft, somewhat abstract allusion to Japanese lanterns and moonlight over Miami.

In the southwest corner is the Challenger Memorial, a monument dedicated to the astronauts killed in the 1986 space-shuttle explosion.

A favorite with the park's youngest visitors is Noguchi's Slide Mantra, a spiral of carrara marble that doubles as a playground piece for the kids.

Yoga in the Park

The Tina Hills Pavilion (admission free), at the south end of the park, is also the setting for free open-air yoga classes. These are held three times a week (Mondays and Wednesdays at 6pm, and 9am Saturday morning) and are suitable for all levels.

Lee & Tina Hills Playground

This playground has soft rubber surfacing and fun climbing toys, slides, and a play area that resembles a ship for pirates (surely every child's favorite villain). The curious sculpture here is a wave containing three of South Florida's wilder residents: a sea turtle, a manatee and a dolphin.

FELIX MIZIOZNIKOV/SHUTTERSTOCK ©

☑ **Top Tips**

▶ Head to the park in the late afternoon and watch the skyscrapers of Downtown light up as the sun goes down.

▶ Tack on a stroll along the nearby Miami Riverwalk for more great waterfront views.

▶ Time your visit to catch an outdoor concert or a free yoga class.

✗ **Take a Break**

Stroll a few blocks west to CVI.CHE105 (p68) for excellent Peruvian fare. Nearby Manna Life Food (p60) is a healthy, eco-friendly snack spot.

Local Life
Downtown & Brickell

The downtown boom is on in Miami, with high-rises sprouting like weeds along the Miami River. Restaurants, fashion boutiques and bars have arrived on the scene, with bold development projects on the horizon. For a taste of what's hot and trendy – from vegan cafes to Balinese-inspired rooftop bars – this trendsetting neighborhood is a great place to explore.

❶ Manna Life Food

This airy, stylish **eatery** (☎786-717-5060; www.mannalifefood.com; 80 NE 2nd Ave; mains $8-12; ☉10am-7pm Mon-Fri, 11am-4pm Sat) has wowed diners with its plant-based menu loaded with superfoods. Filling 'life bowls', arepas and noritos (like a burrito but wrapped with seaweed rather than a tortilla) are packed with flavorful ingredients such as red quinoa, baked tofu, roasted veggies, coconut

brown rice and raw falafel. It's also a good spot for fresh juices, coffees and matcha cappuccinos.

❷ Supply & Advise

Supply & Advise (www.supplyandadvise. com; 223 SE 1st St; ⏱11am-7pm Mon-Sat) brings a heavy dose of men's style to downtown Miami, with rugged, well-made and handsomely tailored clothing plus shoes and accessories set in a historic 1920s building. Most merchandise here is made in the US. There's also a barbershop, complete with vintage chairs and that impeccable look of bygone days.

❸ Bayfront Park

Few American parks can claim to front such a lovely stretch of bright turquoise (Biscayne Bay), but Miamians are lucky like that. This lovely long expanse (p58) that backs into Downtown is the great spot for leisurely waterside walks, picnics and outdoor concerts (which happen from time to time in the on-site amphitheaters).

❹ Miami Riverwalk

This pedestrian walkway follows along the northern edge of the river as it bisects Downtown, and offers some peaceful vantage points of bridges and skyscrapers dotting the urban landscape. You can start the walk at the south end of Bayfront Park and follow it under bridges and along the waterline until it ends just west of the SW 2nd Ave Bridge.

❺ Brickell Avenue Bridge

Crossing the Miami River, the lovely Brickell Avenue Bridge between SE 4th St and SE 5th St was made wider and higher some years back, affording even better views of the Downtown skyline. Note the 17ft bronze statue by Cuban-born sculptor Manuel Carbonell of a Tequesta warrior and his family, which sits atop the towering Pillar of History column.

❻ Brickell City Centre

One of the hottest new developments in Miami finally opened its doors in late 2016, after four long years of construction. There's much to entice both Miami residents and visitors to the **center** (www.brickellcitycentre.com; 701 S Miami Ave; ⏱10am-9:30pm Mon-Sat, noon-7pm Sun), with restaurants, bars, a cinema and loads of high-end retailers (Ted Baker, All Saints, Kendra Scott). You'll find shops scattered across both sides of S Miami Ave between 7th and 8th Sts, including a massive Saks Fifth Ave.

❼ Sugar

One of Miami's hottest **bars** (788 Brickell Plaza, EAST, Miami Hotel, 40th fl; ⏱4pm-1am Mon-Thu, to 3am Fri & Sat, to midnight Sun) of the moment sits on the 40th floor of the EAST, Miami Hotel. Calling it a rooftop bar doesn't quite do the place justice. Verdant oasis is more like it, with a spacious open-air deck full of plants and trees – and sweeping views over the city and Key Biscayne (p90).

Herald Plaza

🚇 5 ▶

Ⓧ 12

Pérez Art Museum Miami

Ⓞ

Museum Park

🚇

Patricia & Phillip Frost 2 Museum of Science Ⓞ

Museum Park

Biscayne Blvd

🚇 26 Ⓞ 28

Adrienne Arsht Center for the Performing Arts Ⓞ

NE 14th St

NE 13th St

NE 12th St

Museum Park

NE 2nd Ave 🚇

11th St Ⓞ

Port Blvd

🚇 Island Queen 7

Bayside Marketplace

Biscayne Blvd

24 🚇

Freedom Tower 6 Ⓞ

1 🚇

🚇 College/ Bayside

Freedom Tower 🚇 College North 🚇

MDC Museum of Art & Design

Park West 🚇

N Miami Ave

8 Ⓧ 21 Ⓘ
19 Ⓞ

NE 10th St

NE 9th St

DOWNTOWN

NE 8th St

NE 7th St

NE 6th St

NE 5th St

N NE 4th St

NE 3rd St

N Miami Ave

Wilkie D Ferguson Jr 🚇

395 🔺

NW 1st Ave 🚇 Overtown

N Miami Ave

NW 1st Ave

NW 1st Ct

NW 2nd Ave

NW 3rd St

Government Center

🚊 Metrorail

500 m
0.25 miles

95

North-South Expwy

NW 10th St

NW 9th St

NW 8th St

NW 4th Ave

NW 8th St

NW 6th St

NW 5th St

NW 4th St

Ⓧ 11 🔻

Lummus Park

NW 3rd Ct

🧭 N

A1A
41

E   D   C   B   A

1   2   3   4

Sights

HistoryMiami　　　MUSEUM

1　◉ Map p62, B5

South Florida – a land of escaped slaves, guerilla Native Americans, gangsters, land grabbers, pirates, tourists, drug dealers and alligators – has a special history, and it takes a special kind of museum to capture that narrative. This highly recommended place, located in the **Miami-Dade Cultural Center**, does just that, weaving together the stories of the region's successive waves of population, from Native Americans to Nicaraguans. (☏305-375-1492; www.historymiami.org; 101 W Flagler St; adult/child $10/5; ◷10am-5pm Mon-Sat, from noon Sun; 🖼)

Patricia & Phillip Frost Museum of Science　　MUSEUM

2　◉ Map p62, D2

This sprawling new Downtown museum spreads across 250,000 sq ft that includes a three-level aquarium, a 250-seat, state-of-the-art planetarium and two distinct wings that delve into the wonders of science and nature. Exhibitions range from weather phenomena to creepy crawlies, feathered dinosaurs and vital-microbe displays, while Florida's fascinating Everglades and biologically rich coral reefs play starring roles. (☏305-434-9600; www.frostscience.org; 1101 Biscayne Blvd; adult/child $28/20; ◷9am-6pm; P🖼)

MDC Museum of Art & Design　　MUSEUM

3　◉ Map p62, D3

Miami-Dade College operates a small but well-curated art museum in Downtown; the permanent collection includes works by Matisse, Picasso and Chagall and focuses on minimalism, pop art and contemporary Latin American art. The museum's home building is art itself: it's set in the soaring 255ft (78m) Freedom Tower, a masterpiece of Mediterranean Revival, built in 1925. (Freedom Tower; ☏305-237-7700; www.mdcmoad.org; 600 Biscayne Blvd)

Miami Center for Architecture & Design　　MUSEUM

4　◉ Map p62, C5

It makes sense that the Miami branch of the American Institute of Architects would pick the Old US Post Office as headquarters of their Center for Architecture & Design. Constructed in 1912, this was the first federal building in Miami. It features a low-pitched roof, elaborate doors and carved entryways, and was purchased in 1937 to serve as the country's first savings and loan association.

Today it houses lectures and events related to architecture, design and urban planning, and hosts a small but vibrant exhibition on all of the above subjects. Two-hour walking tours on alternate Saturdays depart

GALINA SAVINA/SHUTTERSTOCK ©

Freedom Tower

from here (at 10am), and take in some of the historic buildings of Downtown. Visit the website for upcoming times and reservations. (Old US Post Office; ☎305-448-7488; www. miamicad.org; 100 NE 1st Ave; admission free; ☉10am-5pm Mon-Fri)

Miami Children's Museum

MUSEUM

5 ◉ Map p62, E1

This museum, located between South Beach and Downtown Miami, isn't exactly a museum. It feels more like an uberplayhouse, with areas for kids to practice all sorts of adult activities – banking and food shopping, caring for pets, and acting as a local cop

or firefighter. (☎305-373-5437; www. miamichildrensmuseum.org; 980 MacArthur Causeway; $20; ☉10am-6pm; 🚼)

Freedom Tower

HISTORIC BUILDING

6 ◉ Map p62, D3

An iconic slice of Miami's old skyline, the richly ornamented Freedom Tower is one of two surviving towers modeled after the Giralda bell tower in Spain's Cathedral of Seville. As the 'Ellis Island of the South,' it served as an immigration processing center for almost half a million Cuban refugees in the 1960s. Placed on the National Register of Historic Places in 1979, it was also home to the *Miami Daily News* for 32 years.

In the beautifully restored lobby, above the elevators and stretching toward the coffered ceiling, you can see reliefs of men at work on the printing presses. The tower also houses the MDC Museum of Art & Design (p64). (600 Biscayne Blvd; ⊙10am-5pm)

Island Queen
BOATING

 7 Map p62, E3

This outfit runs 90-minute boat tours that take in Millionaire's Row, the Miami River and Fisher Island. There are frequent daily departures (hourly between 11am and 6pm). (☑305-379-5119; www.islandqueencruises.com; 401 Biscayne Blvd; adult/child from $28/20)

Eating

All Day
CAFE $

 8 Map p62, C2

All Day is one of the best places in the Downtown area to linger over coffee or breakfast – no matter the hour. Slender Scandinavian-style chairs, wood-and-marble tables and the Françoise Hardy soundtrack lend an easygoing vibe to the place. (www.alldaymia.com; 1035 N Miami Ave; coffee $3.50, breakfast $10-14; ⊙7am-7pm Mon-Fri, from 9am Sat & Sun; 🛜)

Bali Cafe
INDONESIAN $

9 Map p62, D5

It's odd to think of the clean flavors of sushi and the bright richness of Indonesian cuisine coming together in harmony, but they're happily married in this tropical hole in the wall. Have some spicy tuna rolls for an appetizer, then follow up with *soto betawi* – beef soup cooked with coconut milk, ginger and shallots. (☑305-358-5751; 109 NE 2nd Ave; mains $10-16; ⊙11am-4pm daily, 6-10pm Mon-Fri; 🍴)

La Moon
COLOMBIAN $

 10 Map p62, C8

Nothing hits the spot after a late night of partying quite like a Colombian hot dog topped with eggs and potato sticks. Or an *arepa* (corn cake) stuffed with steak and cheese. These street-food delicacies are available well into the wee hours on weekend nights, plus La Moon is conveniently located within stumbling distance of bars including Blackbird Ordinary (p68).

Top it off with a *refajo*: Colombian beer (Aguila) with Colombian soda (preferably the red one). (☑305-860-6209; www.lamoonrestaurant.com; 97 SW 8th St; mains $7-17; ⊙10am-midnight Sun & Tue-Thu, to 6am Fri & Sat)

Casablanca
SEAFOOD $$

11 Map p62, A4

Perched over the Miami River, Casablanca serves up some of the best seafood in town. The setting is a big draw – with tables on a long wooden deck just above the water, and the odd seagull winging past. But the fresh fish is the real star here. (www.casablancaseafood.com; 400 N River Dr; mains $15-34; ⊙11am-10pm Sun-Thu, to 11pm Fri & Sat)

Verde

AMERICAN $$

12 Map p62, E1

Inside the Pérez Art Museum Miami (p54), Verde is a local favorite for its tasty market-fresh dishes and great setting – with outdoor seating on a terrace overlooking the bay. Crispy mahi-mahi tacos, pizza with squash blossoms and goat cheese, and grilled endive salads are among the temptations. (📞786-345-5697; www.pamm.org/dining; 1103 Biscayne Blvd, Pérez Art Museum Miami; mains $13-19; ⏰Fri-Tue 11am-5pm, to 9pm Thu, closed Wed; 🚇)

River Oyster Bar

SEAFOOD $$

13 Map p62, C7

A few paces from the Miami River, this buzzing little spot with a classy vibe whips up excellent plates of seafood. Start off with their fresh showcase oysters and ceviche before moving on to grilled red snapper or yellowfin tuna. For a decadent meal, go for a grand seafood platter ($125), piled high with Neptune's culinary treasures. (📞305-530-1915; www.therivermiami.com; 650 S Miami Ave; mains $16-32; ⏰noon-10:30pm Mon-Thu, to midnight Fri, 4:30pm-midnight Sat, to 9:30pm Sun)

NIU Kitchen

SPANISH $$

14 Map p62, D5

NIU is a stylish living-room-sized restaurant serving up delectable contemporary Spanish cuisine. It's a showcase of culinary pyrotechnics, with complex sharing plates with clipped Catalan names like Ous (poached eggs, truffled potato foam, *jamon iberico* and black truffle) or Toninya (smoked tuna, green guindillas and pine nuts). Wash it all down with good wine. (📞786-542-5070; www.niukitchen.com; 134 NE 2nd Ave; sharing plates $14-25; ⏰noon-3:30pm & 6-10pm Mon-Fri, 1-4pm & 6-11pm Sat, 6-10pm Sun; 🚇)

PB Station

MODERN AMERICAN $$

15 Map p62, D5

The creative team behind the popular Pubbelly (p36) in Sunset Harbour brought their award-winning formula to Downtown in 2016. Set on the ground floor of the **Langford Hotel** (📞305-250-0782; www.langfordhotelmiami.com; 121 SE 1st St), the dining room channels a classy, old-fashioned elegance with its arched ceilings, globe lights and well-dressed servers. Culinary highlights

Local Life
A Farm-to-Table Dinner

On Monday nights, you can join locals for a delicious five-course vegetarian meal, served family-style at outdoor tables in front of the Arsht Center. **Chef Allen's Farm-to-Table Dinner** (Map p62, D1; 📞786-405-1745; 1300 Biscayne Blvd; dinner $25, with wine pairing $40; ⏰6:30pm Mon; 🚇) is excellent value, with a creative menu inspired by the farmers market held on the same day. Call ahead to reserve a spot.

include bistro classic dishes such as grilled bone marrow, French onion soup and grilled octopus. (☎305-420-2205; http://pbstation.com; 121 SE 1st St, Langford Hotel; mains $20-57; ⊙11:30am-3pm & 6-11pm Mon-Sat)

Soya e Pomodoro   ITALIAN $$

16 🍴 Map p62, D5

Soya e Pomodoro feels like a bohemian retreat for Italian artists and filmmakers, who can dine on bowls of fresh pasta under vintage posters, rainbow paintings and curious wall-hangings. Adding to the vibe is live Latin jazz (on Thursday nights from 9pm to midnight), plus readings and other arts events that take place here on select evenings. (☎305-381-9511; www.soyaepomodoro.com; 120 NE 1st St; lunch $11-18, dinner $16-26; ⊙11:30am-4:30pm Mon-Fri, 7-11:30pm Wed-Sat)

CVI.CHE 105   PERUVIAN $$

17 🍴 Map p62, D5

White is the design element of choice in Juan Chipoco's ever-popular Peruvian Downtown eatery. Beautifully presented ceviches, *lomo saltado* (marinated steak) and *arroz con mariscos* (seafood rice) are ideal for sharing and go down nicely with a round of Pisco Fuegos (made with jalapeño-infused pisco) and other specialty Peruvian cocktails. (☎305-577-3454; www.ceviche105.com; 105 NE 3rd Ave; ⊙noon-10pm Sun-Thu, to 11pm Fri & Sat)

Drinking

Blackbird Ordinary   BAR

18 🍸 Map p62, C7

Far from ordinary, the Blackbird is an excellent bar, with great cocktails (the London Sparrow, with gin, cayenne, lemon juice and passion fruit, goes down well) and an enormous courtyard. The only thing 'ordinary' about the place is the sense that all are welcome for a fun and pretension-free night out. (☎305-671-3307; www.blackbirdordinary.com; 729 SW 1st Ave; ⊙3pm-5am Mon-Fri, 5pm-5am Sat & Sun)

Eleven Miami   CLUB

19 🍸 Map p62, C2

Since its opening way back in 2014, Eleven Miami has remained one of the top Downtown clubs. There's much eye candy here (and we're not talking just about the attractive club-goers): go-go dancers, aerialists and racy (striptease-esque) performances, amid a state-of-the-art sound system, laser lights and video walls, with top DJs working the crowd into a frenzy. (E11EVEN; ☎305-570-4803; www.11miami.com; 29 NE 11th St; ⊙24hr)

Area 31   ROOFTOP BAR

20 🍸 Map p62, D6

On the rooftop of the **Kimpton Epic Hotel** (☎305-424-5226; www.epichotel.com), this buzzing open-air bar draws in the after-work happy-hour crowd, which morphs into a more party-minded

American Airlines Arena (p70)

gathering as the evening progresses. The view – overlooking the river and the high-rises of Downtown – is stunning. (www.area31restaurant.com; 270 Biscayne Blvd Way, Klimpton Epic Hotel; ⏰5-11pm Sun-Thu, to midnight Fri & Sat)

Pawnbroker   ROOFTOP BAR

Head up to the top (penthouse) floor of the Langford Hotel (see 15 ✖ Map p62, D5;) for sweeping views of Downtown, first-rate cocktails and a welcoming, snooty-free vibe. It's a lively spot at happy hour (5pm to 7pm weekdays), when you can catch the sunset, though you won't be alone (go early to beat the crowds). (📞305-420-2200; www.pawnbrokermiami.com; 121

SE 1st St, Langford Hotel; ⏰5pm-midnight Mon-Thu, to 2am Fri & Sat, 4-10pm Sun)

Space   CLUB

21 Map p62, C2

This multilevel warehouse is Miami's main megaclub. With 30,000 sq ft to fill, dancers have room to strut, and an around-the-clock liquor license redefines the concept of after-hours. DJs usually pump each floor with a different sound – hip-hop, Latin, heavy trance – while the infamous rooftop lounge is the place to be for sunrise. (📞305-375-0001; www.clubspace.com; 34 NE 11th St; ⏰11pm-late Fri-Sun)

Level 25   BAR

22 🔘 Map p62, D8

When Neo buys Morpheus a drink, they probably meet at this Conrad Miami spot (guess which floor), where it's all long white lines, low black couches, pin-striped gorgeousity and God's-eye views over Biscayne Bay. (Conrad Miami, 1395 Brickell Ave; ⏱11:30am-11pm Sun-Thu, to midnight Fri & Sat)

Batch Gastropub   BAR

23 🔘 Map p62, C8

This gastropub in Brickell draws a fairly straight-laced crowd. But if you don't mind the slacks and the sports on TV, Batch has appeal: namely a first-rate selection of microbrews and fizzes (carbonated cocktails) on tap, plus creative cocktails and lots of great snacks (truffle fries, grouper tacos, brisket burgers, wild-mushroom pizzas).

There are good food and drink deals during happy hour (weekdays 5pm to 8pm). (www.batchmiami.com; 30 SW 12th St; ⏱noon-3am Sun-Thu, to 4am Fri & Sat)

Entertainment

American Airlines Arena   STADIUM

24 ⭐ Map p62, D3

Resembling a massive spaceship that perpetually hovers at the edge of Biscayne Bay, this arena has been the home of the city's NBA franchise, the Miami Heat, since 2000. The **Waterfront Theater**, Florida's largest, is housed inside; throughout the year it hosts concerts, Broadway performances and the like. (📞786-777-1000; www.aaarena.com; 601 N Biscayne Blvd)

Olympia Theater   PERFORMING ARTS

25 ⭐ Map p62, D5

This elegantly renovated 1920s movie palace services a huge variety of performing arts including film festivals, symphonies, ballets and touring shows. The acoustics are excellent. (📞305-374-2444; www.olympiatheater.org; 174 E Flagler St)

Florida Grand Opera   OPERA

26 ⭐ Map p62, D1

Founded in the 1940s, this highly respected opera company, which stages many shows including *Madame Butterfly*, *La Bohème* and *Tosca*, performs throughout the year at the Adrienne Arsht Center for the Performing Arts and in Fort Lauderdale. (📞800-741-1010; www.fgo.org; 1300 Biscayne Blvd, Adrienne Arsht Center for the Performing Arts)

Miami Hispanic Ballet   DANCE

27 ⭐ Map p62, A6

Directed by Cuban-trained Pedro Pablo Peña, this troupe presents mainly classical ballets based out of the

Public Art

Miami has always been way ahead of the curve when it comes to public art. Miami and Miami Beach established the Art in Public Places program way back in 1973, when it voted to allocate 1.5% of city construction funds to the fostering of public art; since then more than 700 works – sculptures, mosaics, murals, light-based installations and more – have been created in public spots. A series of hand-prints representing Miami's many immigrant communities link into a single community in *Reaching for Miami Skies*, by Connie Lloveras, which greets Metromover commuters at Brickell Station. In Miami-Dade Library, the floating text of *Words Without Thought Never to Heaven Go* by Edward Ruscha challenges readers to engage with the books that surround them. The Argentine duo of Roberto Behar and Rosario Marquardt have been among the most prolific public artists in town, deliberately warping conceptions of what is or isn't public space; they created the giant red M at the Metromover Riverwalk Station for the city's centennial back in 1996.

Miami Hispanic Cultural Arts Center, also known as 'The White House of Ballet.' (☏786-747-1877; www.miamihispanicballet.org; 111 SW 5th Ave)

Shopping

Books & Books BOOKS

28 🔒 Map p62, D1

This excellent bookstore has a small branch in the Adrienne Arsht Center for the Performing Arts. The **cafe** (☏786-405-1745; www.thecafeatbooksandbooks.com; prix-fixe menu $31-35, mains $15-22; ⊙11am-8pm; ☝) is a big draw, as is the small farmers market held on Mondays (from 4pm to 8pm) in front of the store. (1300 Biscayne Blvd, Adrienne Arsht Center for the Performing Arts; ⊙11:30am-8pm)

Mary Brickell Village SHOPPING CENTER

29 🔒 Map p62, C8

This outdoor shopping and dining complex has helped revitalize the Brickell neighborhood, with a range of boutiques, outdoor restaurants, cafes and bars. It's a magnet for new condo residents in the area, with a central location in the heart of the financial district. (☏305-381-6130; www.marybrickellvillage.com; 901 S Miami Ave; ⊙10am-9pm Mon-Sat, noon-6pm Sun)

Explore

Wynwood & the Design District

Wynwood and the Design District are two of Miami's most creative neighborhoods, and justly famed for a burgeoning arts scene. The once industrial wasteland of Wynwood today houses galleries, indie stores, cafes and restaurants, plus an incredible array of street art. The smaller Design District also has galleries, plus high-end shopping and a mixed bag of bars and eateries.

The Sights in a Day

☀️ Start off the with freshly-baked goodies at **Zak the Baker** (p82), followed by a quality brew at **Panther Coffee** (p82). Next stroll down to the **Wynwood Walls** (p74), to see massive works of art covering a former industrial strip. For more great art, check out some of the galleries sprinkled around Wynwood. Many places are free, while others – such as the stellar **Margulies Collection at the Warehouse** (p80) – are well worth the entry fee.

☀️ For lunch head up to the Design District to **Lost & Found Saloon** (p84) for satisfying Tex-Mex in a whimsical setting. Afterwards take a stroll around the neighborhood for a look at public art installations, galleries and high-end boutiques.

🌙 In the evening, make your back down to Wynwood to see the neighborhood at its liveliest. Reserve a table at **Alter** (p84), one of the district's top restaurants, drink a one-of-a-kind microbrew at **Boxelder** (p86), then head up to **Lagniappe** (p84) for a bit of live music in a charming backyard setting.

For a local's day in the Design District, see p76

👁 Top Sight

Wynwood Walls (p74)

◯ Local Life

Art & High Design (p76)

🖤 Best of Miami

Eating
Kyu (p83)

Alter (p84)

Kush (p82)

Drinking
Lagniappe (p84)

Wynwood Brewing Company (p85)

Bardot (p85)

Shopping
Nomad Tribe (p86)

Frangipani (p87)

Malaquita (p87)

Getting There

🚋 **Trolley** Biscayne Trolley runs up Brickell Ave, Biscayne, 29th St and 39th St. Wynwood Trolley goes from 15th St near the Adrienne Arsht Center over to NW 2nd Ave.

🚌 **Bus** From South Beach, take bus 120 down Washington Ave over to Miami and transfer at the Adrienne Arsht Center to a Trolley.

Top Sights
Wynwood Walls

The launch of the Wynwood Walls was like a meteor soaring through the upper atmosphere of the art world. It came in the form of eye-popping, color-saturated murals blanketing the walls of a former warehouse district. Artists from around the world have added their touch to this ever-changing open-air gallery, transforming Wynwood into a mecca for art lovers.

Map p79, B6

www.thewynwoodwalls.com

NW 2nd Ave btwn 25th & 26th Sts

admission free

Back Story

During the early 2000s, there wasn't much happening in Wynwood. Ever since the 1970s, Wynwood had been known as little more than a district of warehouses. And then Tony Goldman arrived.

Goldman, who's credited with the revitalization of South Beach (as well as New York's SoHo district), saw potential in the blighted neighborhood. He bought up properties. Once assembled, he unleashed his master plan and invited international artists to create the biggest and boldest collection of street art ever assembled in Miami.

The launch in 2009 was a smash success. That year at **Art Basel** (www.artbasel.com/miami-beach; ⓦearly Dec), thousands of visitors came to see the street murals, and the new Wynwood Walls were the talk of the town.

The Art

One of the most extraordinary features of the Wynwood Walls is that nothing here remains the same – which is perhaps an appropriate metaphor for the ephemeral nature of street art in general. The average lifespan for a mural here is less than one year before it's painted over by another artist – surprising given the stunning quality of work on display. Since the founding of the project, more than 50 artists from 16 different countries have painted on the walls.

Museum of the Streets

The Walls are the heart of Wynwood's open-air gallery, but it is no longer the only game in town. After Goldman's success, other property owners invited artists to paint the walls of their buildings. Within a few years, the whole neighborhood became one giant street museum – one that presents constant surprises at every turn, and endless opportunities to capture great street photography.

☑ **Top Tips**

▸ Go early in the day to beat the crowds.

▸ Wynwood Walls offers private walking tours ($25 per person) led by street artists. Book online.

▸ You can learn more about the neighborhood's street art and its gallery scene on a walking tour offered by Wynwood Art Walk (p82).

▸ A great time to see the neighborhood at its most celebratory is during the Wynwood Art Walk (p82), held on the second Saturday of the month.

✗ **Take a Break**

Grab some delicious Mexican-style street food at Coyo Taco (p80). Stay caffeinated at Panther Coffee (p82), serving the best pour-overs in Miami.

Local Life
Art & High Design

One neighborhood that more than lives up to its name is the Design District, a compact area sprinkled with galleries, stylish eateries and high-end designer boutiques. Aside from luxury retailers, you'll find some lovely contemporary architecture throughout, along with intriguing outdoor installations that bring the art out of the gallery and into the public sphere. The main drags are along NW 39th and 40th Sts.

❶ Locust Projects

Locust Projects (☏305-576-8570; www.locustprojects.org; 3852 N Miami Ave; admission free; ☉10am-6pm Tue-Sat) has become a major name for emerging artists in the contemporary gallery scene. Run by artists as a non profit collective since 1998, LP has exhibited work by more than 250 local, national and international artists over the years. The gallery often hosts site-specific installations by artists and is

willing to take a few more risks than more commercial venues.

❷ Palm Court

At the epicenter of the design district is this pretty **courtyard** (140 NE 39th St), which opened just before Art Basel back in 2014. It's set with tall palm trees, two floors of high-end retailers and one eye-catching sculpture. The Fly's Eye Dome is a geodesic dome that appears to be floating (or gently submerged) in a square fountain.

❸ Crumb on Parchment

When you need a pick-me-up or have a craving for something sweet, there's no better place to be than this outrageously good cafe and **bakery** (☑305-572-9444; 3930 NE 2nd Ave; mains $9-15; ☉9am-4pm Mon-Fri; 🛜🍴). Aside from rich chocolate brownies, scones and other baked goods, the charming sun-drenched cafe serves up inventive sandwiches, salads and soups.

❹ The Bazaar Project

In the Design District, this is a fun **store** (☑786-703-6153; www.thebazaar projectshop.com; 4308 NE 2nd Ave; ☉11am-8pm Mon-Sat, noon-6pm Sun) for a browse, with curious objects that may or may not fit in your suitcase. You'll find throw pillows with photorealistic images of wild animals, ceramic dishes that blend European and Asian styles, pencil holders disguised as vintage SLR cameras, skull-shaped candles and one-of-a-kind fragrances by Mancera.

❺ Michael's Genuine

The liveliest place in the Design District is this long-running upscale **tavern** (☑305-573-5550; www.michaelsgenuine. com; 130 NE 40th St; mains lunch $16-26, dinner $19-44; ☉11:30am-11pm Mon-Sat, to 10pm Sun) that combines excellent service with a well-executed menu of wood-fired dishes, bountiful salads and raw bar temptations (including oysters and stone crabs). It tends to draw a well-dressed crowd, and the place gets packed most days. There's also outdoor dining on the pedestrian strip out front.

❻ Living Room

Reminding you that you're entering the Design District is a surreal public art installation of, yep, a living room – just the sort of thing you're supposed to shop for while here. Actually this **Living Room** (cnr NW 40th St & N Miami Ave), by Argentine couple Roberto Behar and Rosario Marquardt, is an 'urban intervention' meant to be a criticism of the disappearance of public space.

❼ De La Cruz Collection

This 30,000-sq-ft **gallery** (☑305-576-6112; www.delacruzcollection.org; 23 NE 41st St; admission free; ☉10am-4pm Tue-Sat) has a treasure trove of contemporary works scattered across three floors, which you can roam freely. Rosa and Carlos de la Cruz, who originally hail from Cuba, have particularly strong holdings in postwar German paintings, as well as fascinating works by Jim Hodges, Ana Mendieta and Felix Gonzalez Torres.

Biscayne Blvd

NE 4th Ct
NE 4th Ave

1

27
13
22

NE 2nd Ave
East Coast Ave

E

11
NE 2nd Ave

NE 46th St

NE 48th St

DESIGN
DISTRICT

NE 1st Ave

NE 40th St

195

112

NE 36th St

Midtown
Miami

NE 1st Ave

NW 34th St

D

N Miami Ave

N Miami Ave

19

Art 3
Fusion

24

NW 33rd St

NW 32nd St

NW 48th St

NW 47th Tce

NW 47th St

NW 46th St

NW 45th St

NW 44th St

NW 42nd St

NW 1st Ave

NW 39th St

NW 38th St

NW 37th St

20

NW 35th St

Roberto
Clemente
Park

WYNWOOD

C

NW 2nd Ave

NW 41st St

NW 40th St

NW 3rd Ave

NW 3rd Ave

27

NW 5th St

NW 5th Ave

B

NW 5th Ave

NW 36th St

NW 35th St

2 Bakehouse
Art Complex

NW 6th Ave

500 m
0.25 miles

95

441

112

Allapattah M
(0.5mi)

30

NW 7th Ave

A

N

4

3

2

1

Biscayne Blvd

NE 2nd Ave

NE 23rd St

NE 22nd St

NE 21st St

NE 20th St

NE 19th St

14

32

NE 29th St

7

N Miami Ave

NW Miami Ct

NW Miami Ct

4

12

8

27

6

NW 1st Ave

NW 18th St

NW 31st St

NW 30th St

NW 28th St

NW 27th St

NW 26th St

NW 25th St

NW 24th St

NW 23rd St

NW Miami Ct

NW 1st Ct

NW 1st Ct

16

34

26

18

31

35

NW 1st Pl

33

10

NW 2nd Ave

NW 2nd Ave

15

21

5

29

9

25

Wynwood Walls

NW 24th St

NW 23rd St

NW 22nd La

NW 22nd St

NW 20th St

NW 19th St

17

1 Margulies Collection at the Warehouse

28

NW 5th Ave

23

NW 6th Ave

95

NW 29th St

NW 7th Ave

NW 23rd St

NW 7th Ave

441

Santa Clara (0.4mi)

NW 21st St

Sights

Margulies Collection at the Warehouse
GALLERY

1 Map p78, B6

Encompassing 45,000 sq ft, this vast not-for-profit exhibition space houses one of the best collections in Wynwood. Thought-provoking, large-format installations are the focus at the Warehouse, and you'll see works by some leading 21st-century artists here. (☏305-576-1051; www.margulieswarehouse.com; 591 NW 27th St; adult/student $10/5; ⏰11am-4pm Tue-Sat mid-Oct–Apr)

Bakehouse Art Complex
GALLERY

2 ◉ Map p78, B4

One of the pivotal art destinations in Wynwood, the Bakehouse has been an arts incubator since well before the creation of the Wynwood Walls. Today this former bakery houses galleries and some 60 studios, and the range of works you can find here is quite impressive. Check the schedule for upcoming artist talks and other events. (BAC; ☏305-576-2828; www.bacfl.org; 561 NW 32nd St; admission free; ⏰noon-5pm; P)

Art Fusion
GALLERY

3 ◉ Map p78, D3

This sprawling gallery in Midtown carries a hugely varied collection, with artists from around the globe. You'll find sculpture, portraiture, landscapes and mixed media spread across two floors of the 8000-sq-ft space. (www.artfusionartists.com; 3550 N Miami Ave; admission free; ⏰11am-6pm Mon-Sat)

Eating

Della Test Kitchen
VEGAN $

4 🍴 Map p78, D5

From a food truck parked in Wynwood Yard, this place offers delicious 'bowls' – build-your-own culinary works of art featuring ingredients such as black coconut rice, ginger tempeh, chickpeas, sweet potato and marinated kale. It's heavenly good and quite healthy. Not surprisingly, DTK has quite a following. (☏305-351-2961; www.dellabowls.com; 56 NW 29th St, Wynwood Yard; mains $11-14; ⏰noon-10pm Tue-Sun; 🍴)

Coyo Taco
MEXICAN $

5 🍴 Map p78, C6

If you're in Wynwood and craving tacos, this is the place to be. You'll have to contend with lines day or night, but those beautifully turned-out tacos are well worth the wait – and come in creative varieties such as chargrilled octopus, marinated mushrooms or crispy duck, along with the usual array of steak, grilled fish and roasted pork. (☏305-573-8228; www.coyo-taco.com; 2300 NW 2nd Ave; mains $7-12; ⏰11am-2am Mon-Sat, to 11pm Sun; 🍴)

JOAQUIN BARBARA/SHUTTERSTOCK ©

Zak the Baker (p83)

Salty Donut

DOUGHNUTS $

6 Map p78, D6

Although 'artisanal doughnuts' sounds pretentious, no one can deny the merits of these artfully designed creations featuring seasonal ingredients – probably the best in South Florida. Maple and bacon, guava and cheese, and brown butter and salt are a few classics, joined by changing hits such as pistachio and white chocolate or strawberry and lemon cream. (☏305-925-8126; www.saltydonut. com; 50 NW 23rd St; doughnuts $3-6; ◷8am-6pm Tue-Sun; ☏)

SuViche

FUSION $

7 Map p78, D5

SuViche is a great place to start off the night, with a buzzing open-sided setting of garrulous couples chatting over swinging chairs, graffiti-esque murals and good beats. The menu is a blend of Peruvian dishes (including half a dozen varieties of ceviche) and sushi, which goes down nicely with the creative *macerados* (pisco-infused cocktails). (☏305-501-5010; www.suviche. com; 2751 N Miami Ave; ceviche $8-14; ◷noon-11pm)

Local Life
Monthly Art Fest

One of the best ways to take in the burgeoning Miami art scene is to join in the **Wynwood Art Walk** (Map p79, E8; www.artcircuits.com; admission free; ⊙7-10pm 2nd Sat of the month), held on the second Saturday of every month. Many of the galleries around Wynwood host special events and art openings, with ever-flowing drinks (not always free), live music around the 'hood, food trucks and special markets.

Kush
AMERICAN $

8 Map p78, D7

Gourmet burgers plus craft brews is the simple but winning formula at this lively eatery and drinking den on the southern fringe of Wynwood. Juicy burgers topped with hot pastrami, Florida avocados and other decadent options go down nicely with drafts from Sixpoint and Funky Buddha. There are great vegetarian options too, including a house-made black-bean burger and vegan jambalaya. (☑305-576-4500; www.kushwynwood.com; 2003 N Miami Ave; mains $13-15; ⊙noon-11pm Sun-Tue, to midnight Wed-Sat; ✏)

Zak the Baker
BAKERY $

9 Map p78, C6

Everyone's favorite bakery has become a Miami icon, and for good reason. The fresh baked breads, croissants and pastries are fabulous. For something more filling, don't miss ZTB's Deli (p83) up the street. (☑786-294-0876; www.zakthebaker.com; 295 NW 26th St; pastries from $3.50; ⊙7am-5pm Sun-Fri)

Panther Coffee
CAFE $

10 Map p78, C6

Miami's best independent coffee shop specializes in single-origin, small-batch roasts, fired up to perfection. Aside from sipping on a zesty brewed-to-order Chemex-made coffe e (or a creamy latte), you can enjoy micro-brews, wines and sweet treats. The front patio is a great spot for people-watching. (☑305-677-3952; www.panthercoffee.com; 2390 NW 2nd Ave; coffees $3-6; ⊙7am-9pm Mon-Sat, from 8am Sun; 🛜)

Buena Vista Deli
CAFE $

11 Map p78, E1

Never mind the uninspiring name: French-owned Buena Vista Deli is a charming Parisian-style cafe that warrants a visit no matter the time of day. Come in the morning for fresh croissants and other bakery temptations, and later in the day for thick slices of quiche, big salads and hearty sandwiches – plus there's wine, beer and good coffees. (☑305-576-3945; www.buenavistadeli.com; 4590 NE 2nd Ave; mains $8-15; ⊙7am-9pm)

Ono Poke
HAWAIIAN $

12 Map p78, D6

This popular little eatery has been all the rage since its 2016 debut. The key to success is all in the execution: diners build their own *poke* bowl, featuring mouthwateringly fresh sushi-grade fish, then place atop greens or rice, and add toppings (ginger, cucumber, scallion), creative extras (wasabi peas), sauce of choice and enjoy – a delicious, nutritious, but refreshingly uncomplicated meal. (☏ 786-618-5366; www.onopokeshop.com; 2320 N Miami Ave; mains $10-16; ☉noon-8pm Mon-Sat, to 6pm Sun)

La Latina
LATIN AMERICAN $

13 Map p78, E4

One of the best budget meals near the Design District can be found at La Latina, a Venezuelan diner that's popular with Midtown locals and artsy transplants to the area. Cheese and avocado *arepas* (corn cakes) are a treat for vegetarians, but there's a lot of meat, rice, beans and sweet plantains filling out the menu. (☏ 305-571-9655; www.lalatinamiami.com; 3509 NE 2nd Ave; mains $6-10; ☉10am-10pm Sun-Thu, to 5am Fri & Sat; ⚲)

Enriqueta's
LATIN AMERICAN $

14 Map p78, E5

Back in the day, Puerto Ricans, not installation artists, ruled Wynwood. Have a taste of those times in this perpetually packed roadhouse, where the Latin-diner ambience is as strong as the steaming shots of *cortadito* (half espresso and half milk) served at the counter. Balance the local gallery fluff with a juicy Cuban sandwich. (☏ 305-573-4681; 186 NE 29th St; mains $6-9; ☉6am-3:45pm Mon-Fri, to 2pm Sat)

Kyu
FUSION $$

15 Map p78, C6

One of the best new restaurants in Wynwood, Kyu has been dazzling locals and food critics alike with its creative, Asian-inspired dishes, most of which are cooked up over the open flames of a wood-fired grill. The buzzing, industrial space is warmed up via artful lighting and wood accents (tables and chairs, plus shelves of firewood for the grill). (☏786-577-0150; www.kyumiami.com; 251 NW 25th St; sharing plates $17-38; ☉noon-11:30pm Mon-Sat, 11am-10:30pm Sun, bar till 1am Fri & Sat; ⚲)

Cake Thai
THAI $$

16 Map p78, C5

When cravings for Thai food strike, Wynwooders no longer need to make the trek up to 79th St and Biscayne (Cake Thai's tiny original location). Now they've got expertly prepared Thai cooking right in their backyard, with all of the same culinary wizardry of chef Phuket Thongsodchaveondee (who goes by the name 'Cake'). (☏305-573-5082; www.cakethaimiami.com; 180 NW 29th St; mains $16-25; ☉noon-midnight Tue-Sun; ⚲)

Zak the Baker
DELI $$

17 Map p78, B6

Miami's best-loved kosher deli is admired by all for its delicious (but pricey) sandwiches: try the braised, handcut corned beef or a satisfying gravlax sandwich. You can also come early for potato latkes and eggs.

(☎786-347-7100; www.zakthebaker.com; 405 NW 26th St; sandwiches $14-18; ⏰8am-5pm Sun-Fri)

Butcher Shop

AMERICAN $$

18 ✕ Map p78, C6

This is called the Butcher Shop for a reason, and that's because it's shamedly aimed at carnivores. From bone-in rib eyes to smoked sausages to full charcuterie, meat lovers have reason to rejoice. Beer lovers too: this butcher doubles as a beer garden, which gets lively as the sun goes down. (☎305-846-9120; www.butchershopmiami.com/tbs; 165 NW 23rd St; mains $13-34; ⏰11am-11pm Sun-Thu, to 2am Fri & Sat)

Harry's Pizzeria

PIZZA $$

19 ✕ Map p78, D3

A stripped-down yet sumptuous dining experience awaits (pizza) pie lovers in the Design District. Harry's tiny kitchen and dining room dishes out deceptively simple wood-fired pizzas topped with creative ingredients (like slow-roasted pork or kale and caramelized onion). Add in some not-to-be missed appetizers like polenta fries and you have a great, budget-friendly meal. (☎786-275-4963; www.harryspizzeria.com; 3918 N Miami Ave; pizzas $13-17, mains $16-21; ⏰11:30am-10pm Sun-Thu, to midnight Fri & Sat; ✎)

Lost & Found Saloon

MEXICAN $$

20 ✕ Map p78, C3

The service is friendly and the cooking is first-rate at this lively little Wynwood saloon. The kitschy southwest-themed joint (with wagon-wheel chandeliers and poker-faced cowboy cut-outs) makes a fine setting for pulled-pork sandwiches, breakfast tacos and, uh, chipotle tofu melts (never mind whether a leering John Wayne would approve). (☎305-576-1008; www.thelostandfoundsaloon-miami .com; 185 NW 36th St; mains $10-20; ⏰11am-3am; ✎)

Alter

MODERN AMERICAN $$$

21 ✕ Map p78, C6

This new spot, which has garnered much praise from food critics, brings creative high-end cooking to Wynwood courtesy of its award-winning young chef Brad Kilgore. The changing menu showcases Florida's high-quality ingredients from sea and land in seasonally inspired dishes with Asian and European accents. Reserve ahead. (☎305-573-5996; www. altermiami.com; 223 NW 23rd St; set menu 5/7 courses $69/89; ⏰7-11pm Tue-Sun)

Drinking

Lagniappe

BAR

22 🍷 Map p78, E4

A touch of New Orleans in Miami, Lagniappe has an old-fashioned front room bar, packed with art, faded vintage furnishings and weathered walls. The vibe is just right: with great live music (nightly from 9pm to midnight) and an easygoing crowd, plus there's a sprawling back garden with palm trees and fairy lights. (☎305-576-0108; www.lagniappehouse. com; 3425 NE 2nd Ave; ☺7pm-2am Sun-Thu, to 3am Fri & Sat)

Wynwood Brewing Company
MICROBREWERY

23 Map p78, B6

The beer scene has grown in leaps and bounds in Miami, but this warmly lit spot, which was the first craft brewery in Wynwood, is still the best. The family-owned 15-barrel brewhouse has friendly and knowledgeable staff, excellent year-round brews (including a blonde ale, a robust porter and a top-notch IPA) and seasonal beers, and there's always a food truck parked outside. (☎305-982-8732; www.wynwoodbrewing.com; 565 NW 24th St; ☺noon-10pm Sun & Mon, to midnight Tue-Sat)

Bardot
CLUB

24 Map p78, D4

You really should see the interior of Bardot before you leave the city. It's all sexy French vintage posters and furniture (plus a pool table) seemingly plucked from a private club that serves millionaires by day, and becomes a scene of decadent excess by night. The entrance looks to be on N Miami Ave, but it's actually in a parking lot behind the building. (☎305-576-5570; www.bardotmiami.com; 3456 N Miami Ave; ☺8pm-3am Tue & Wed, to 5am Thu-Sat)

Top Tip

Food Trucks & Cocktails

On a once vacant lot, the **Wynwood Yard** (Map p79, D5; www.thewynwoodyard. com; 56 NW 29th St; mains $7-14; ☺noon-11pm Tue-Thu, to 1am Fri-Sun; 🛜🍴) is something of an urban oasis for those who want to enjoy a bit of casual open-air eating and drinking. Around a dozen different food trucks park here, offering gourmet mac and cheese, cruelty-free salads, meaty schnitzel plates, zesty tacos, desserts and more. There's also a bar, and often live music.

Coyo Taco
BAR

Secret bars hidden behind taco stands are all the rage in Miami these days. To find this one, head inside Coyo Taco (see 5 ❌ Map p78, C6), down the corridor past the bathrooms and enter the unmarked door. Inside you'll find a classy low-lit spot with elaborate ceramic tile floors, a long wooden bar and a DJ booth, with brassy Latin rhythms and Afro Cuban funk filling the space. (www.coyo-taco.com; 2300 NW 2nd Ave; ☺5pm-midnight Sun-Wed, to 3am Thu-Sat)

Concrete Beach Brewery
BREWERY

25 Map p78, C6

Concrete Beach is a great little neighborhood brewery, with a gated courtyard where you can linger over hoppy IPAs, wheat beers with a hint of citrus, and easy-drinking pilsners, plus seasonal brews (like a juniper saison called Miami Gras, which typically launches in February). It's not always the liveliest spot, but a fine stop for beer connoisseurs. (📞305-796-2727; www. concretebeachbrewery.com; 325 NW 24th St; ⏱5-11pm Mon-Thu, to 1am Fri, from 1pm Sat & Sun)

Gramps

BAR

26 🍺 Map p78, C6

Friendly and unpretentious (just like some grandpas), Gramps always has something afoot whether it's live music and DJs (Fridays and Saturdays), trivia and bingo nights (Tuesdays and Wednesdays) or straight-up karaoke (Thursdays). The big draw though is really just the sizable backyard that's perfect for alfresco drinking and socializing. (📞786-752-6693; www.gramps.com; 176 NW 24th St; ⏱11am-1am Sun-Wed, to 3am Thu-Sat)

Local Life
Boxelder

This long, narrow space (Map p78, C5) is a beer-lover's Valhalla, with a brilliantly curated menu of brews from near and far, though its 20 rotating beer taps leave pride of place for South Florida beers. There's also more than 100 different varieties by the bottle. What keeps the place humming is Boxelder's friendly, down-to-earth vibe.

Entertainment

O Cinema Wynwood

CINEMA

27 ⭐ Map p78, D5

This much-loved nonprofit cinema screens indie films, foreign films and documentaries. You'll find intriguing works you won't see elsewhere. (📞305-571-9970; www.o-cinema.org; 90 NW 29th St)

Light Box at Goldman Warehouse

PERFORMING ARTS

28 ⭐ Map p78, B6

The Miami Light Project, a nonprofit cultural foundation, stages a wide range of innovative theater, dance, music and film performances at this intimate theater. It's a great place to discover cutting-edge works by artists you might not have heard of. They're particularly supportive of troupes from South Florida. (📞305-576-4350; www. miamilightproject.com; 404 NW 26th St)

Shopping

Nomad Tribe

CLOTHING

29 🔒 Map p78, C6

This boutique carrys only ethically and sustainably produced merchandise. You'll find cleverly designed jewelry from Miami-based Kathe Cuervo, Osom brand socks (made of upcycled thread), ecologically produced graphic T-shirts from Thinking MU, and THX coffee and candles (which donates 100% of profits to nonprofit organizations) among much else.

(📞305-364-5193; www.nomadtribeshop.
com; 2301 NW 2nd Ave; ⊘noon-8pm)

Brooklyn Vintage & Vinyl   MUSIC

30 🔒 Map p78, A4

Only opened in late 2016, this record
store has already attracted a following.
It's mostly vinyl (plus some cassettes
and a few T-shirts), with around 5000
records in the inventory. Staff can give
good tips for exploring new music.
(www.facebook.com/brooklynvintageandvinyl;
3454 NW 7th Ave; ⊘noon-9pm Tue-Sat)

Shinola   FASHION & ACCESSORIES

31 🔒 Map p78, C6

This dapper little store by the Detroit-
based Shinola proves that American
manufacturing is far from dead. Shinola makes beautifully crafted watches,
wallets, journals, pens, bicycles and
even limited-edition turntables. The
prices can be rather staggering, but its
all of the highest quality. (📞786-374-
2994; www.shinola.com; 2399 NW 2nd Ave;
⊘11am-7pm Mon-Sat, noon-6pm Sun; 🛜)

Art by God   GIFTS & SOUVENIRS

32 🔒 Map p78, D6

Take a walk on the wild side at this
sprawling warehouse full of relics of
days past. Fossils, minerals and semi-
precious stones play supporting roles to
the more eye-catching draws: full-size
giraffes, lions, bears and zebras in all
their taxidermied glory. (📞305-573-3011;
www.artbygod.com; 60 NE 27th St; ⊘10am-
5pm Mon-Fri, 11am-4pm Sat)

Frangipani   ARTS & CRAFTS

33 🔒 Map p78, C6

You'll find great gift ideas at this inviting little shop on Wynwood's busiest
thoroughfare. Handmade napkins,
vintage Berber baskets, etched drinking
glasses (also Moroccan), one-of-a-kind
notecards and stationery, cute toddler
clothes, collage-making boxes and other
crafty kits for kids, plus jewelry, handbags and skincare products. (📞305-573-
1480; www.frangipanimiami.com; 2516 NW 2nd
Ave; ⊘11am-7pm)

Malaquita   ARTS & CRAFTS

34 🔒 Map p78, C6

This artfully designed store has
merchandise you won't find elsewhere,
including lovely handblown vases,
embroidered clothing, Mesoamerican
tapestries, vibrantly painted bowls,
handwoven palm baskets and other
fair-trade objects – some of which are
made by indigenous artisans in Mexico.
(www.malaquitadesign.com; 2613 NW 2nd Ave;
⊘11am-7pm)

Base   CLOTHING

35 🔒 Map p78, C7

Base is a stylish menswear boutique
with handsomely tailored button-
downs and well-fitting pants, Herschel
bags and satchels, minimalist neck-
laces, high-end grooming products
and eye-catching magazines (*Tapas*,
Kinfolk) that seem to perfectly embody
the Base lifestyle brand. (www.baseworld.
com; 2215 NW 2nd Ave; ⊘11am-7pm)

Local Life
Upper East Side

Northeast of Wynwood, the Upper East Side is something of Miami's great new frontier, with creative shops, art studios and cafes opening up here in the last few years. There's plenty of hidden surprises here from a great Eastern European market to secret kayaking spots on the bay.

Getting There

🚌 Several buses run along Biscayne Blvd, including routes 3, 16 and 93, which you can catch on 29th St near Wynwood. From Downtown, take bus 93. From Mid-Beach, take bus 112.

❶ Morningside Park

This aptly named waterfront **park** (750 NE 55 Tce) is a great spot to be in the morning. There's lots going on here, with basketball courts, tennis courts, sports fields, a playground for kids and a swimming pool (admission $3). If you come on Saturday, you can hire kayaks (from $12 per hour) and stand-up paddleboards (from $20 per hour).

❷ Upper East Side Farmers Market

For a taste of local culture, stop by this small **farmers market** (cnr Biscayne Blvd & 66th St, Legion Park; ⏱9am-2pm Sat) held each Saturday in the Upper East Side's Legion Park. Here you can buy fresh fruits, veggies, breads, crackers, pastries, cheeses, jams, honeys and fresh juices. In short, everything you need for a great picnic. It's open year-round.

❸ Kundalini Yoga

This **yoga studio** (☎305-603-8540; www.kymiami.com; 6901 Biscayne Blvd; drop-in class $20, mat rental $2; ⏱10am-6:30pm Mon-Sat, to 4pm Sun) gets high marks for its classes, which have quite a local following. As with other Kundalini centers, there's very much a spiritual, meditative aspect to the practice here.

❹ Vagabond Hotel

An icon in the MiMo (Miami Modern) district, the **Vagabond** (☎305-400-8420; www.thevagabondhotel.com; 7301 Biscayne Blvd) is a 1953 motel and restaurant where Frank Sinatra and other Rat Packers used to hang out. Today it's been reborn as a boutique hotel, and has lost none of its allure. There's also a great **bar** (www.vagabondkitchenandbar.com; ⏱5-11pm Sun-Thu, to midnight Fri & Sat) fronting the hidden pool in back – well worth returning to later in the evening.

❺ Miami Ironside

A new hub of creativity is this urban **oasis** (www.miamiironside.com; 7610 NE 4th Ct) in an otherwise industrial 'hood known as Little River. Here you'll find art and design studios, showrooms and galleries as well as eating and drinking spaces. It's a lushly landscaped property, with some intriguing public art.

❻ Marky's Gourmet

A Miami institution among Russians, Russophiles and those who simply love to explore global cuisine, **Marky's** (☎305-758-9288; www.markys.com; 687 NE 79th St; ⏱9am-7pm Mon-Fri, 10am-6pm Sat, to 5pm Sun) has been going strong since 1983. Foodies from afar flock here to load up on gourmet cheeses, olives, European-style sausages, wines, cakes, teas, jams, chocolates, caviar and more.

❼ The Anderson

The Anderson (www.theandersonmiami.com; 709 NE 79th St; ⏱5pm-2am Sun-Thu, to 4am Fri & Sat) is a great neighborhood bar with a dimly lit interior sprinkled with red couches, animal-print fabrics, wild wallpaper and a glittering jukebox. Head to the back patio for more of a tropical-themed setting where you can dip your toes in the sand (never mind the absent oceanfront).

Local Life
Key Biscayne

Key Biscayne and neigh-boring Virginia Key are a quick and easy getaway from Downtown Miami. But once you've passed across those scenic causeways, you'll feel like you've been transported to a far-off tropical realm, with magnificent beaches, lush nature trails in state parks, and aquatic adventures aplenty.

Getting There

🚌 Number 102 provides service from Brickell (near Brickell Station on SW 1st Ave) over the Rickenbacker Causeway and all the way down to the Bill Baggs Cape Florida State Park.

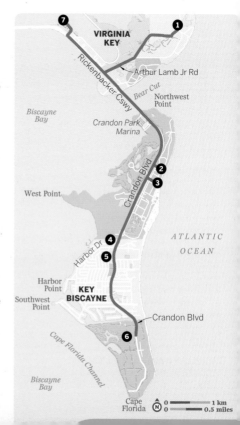

1 Virginia Key Beach
North Point Park

This lovely green **space** (3801 Rickenbacker Causeway, Virginia Key; per vehicle weekday/weekend $6/8; ⏰7am-6pm) has several small beaches and short nature trails. The big reason for coming here is to get out on the water by hiring kayaks or stand-up paddleboards at Virginia Key Outdoor Center.

2 Marjory Stoneman Douglas
Biscayne Nature Center

This child-friendly **nature center** (☎305-361-6767; www.biscaynenaturecenter.org; 6767 Crandon Blvd, Crandon Park; admission free; ⏰10am-4pm; P 🚻) is a great introduction to South Florida's unique ecosystems, with hands-on exhibits and aquariums full of local marine life. You can also stroll a nature trail through coastal hammock (hardwood forest) or enjoy the beach in front.

3 Crandon Park

This 1200-acre park boasts **Crandon Park Beach** (☎305-361-5421; www.miami-dade.gov/parks/parks/crandon_beach.asp; 6747 Crandon Blvd; per car weekday/weekend $5/7; ⏰sunrise-sunset; P 🚻 🐕), a glorious stretch of sand that spreads for 2 miles. The beach here is clean, not cluttered with tourists, faces a lovely sweep of teal goodness and is named one of the best beaches in the USA.

4 Oasis

This excellent **Cuban cafe** (☎305-361-9009; 19 Harbor Dr; mains $8-12; ⏰8am-9pm) has a customer base that ranges from the working poor to city players, and

the socioeconomic barriers come tumbling down fast as folks sip high-octane Cuban coffee. Try the decadent, meaty Cuban sandwiches or the home-style cooking of platters of pork, rice and beans and deep-fried plantains.

5 La Boulangerie Boul'Mich

This delightful French-style **bakery** (www.laboulangerieusa.com; 328 Crandon Blvd; mains $12-15, pastries $3-6; ⏰7:30am-8pm Mon-Sat, 8am-3pm Sun; 📶🍴) whips up delicious quiches, satisfying veggie- or meat-filled empanadas, heavenly pastries, and of course buttery croissants.

6 Bill Baggs Cape
Florida State Park

If you don't make it to the Florida Keys, come to this **park** (☎305-361-5811; www.floridastateparks.org/capeflorida; 1200 S Crandon Blvd; per car/person $8/2; ⏰8am-sunset, lighthouse 9am-5pm; P 🚻 🐕) for a taste of its unique island ecosystems. The 494-acre space is a tangled clot of tropical fauna and dark mangroves, all interconnected by sandy trails and wooden boardwalks.

7 Rusty Pelican

It's often the panoramic skyline views that draw the faithful and romantic to the **Pelican** (☎305-361-3818; www.therustypelican.com; 3201 Rickenbacker Causeway, Virginia Key; mains lunch $13-18, dinner $29-44; ⏰11am-11pm Sun-Thu, to midnight Fri & Sat). But if you come for a sunset drink, the fresh air could certainly seduce you into staying for some of the surf 'n' turf menu, which is packed with high-end grilled steaks and seafood.

Explore

Little Havana

Little Havana's main thoroughfare, Calle Ocho (SW 8th St), doesn't just cut through the heart of the neighborhood; it *is* the heart of the neighborhood. Admittedly, the Cubaness of Little Havana is slightly exaggerated for visitors, though it's still an atmospheric place to explore, with the crack of dominoes, the scent of wafting cigars, and Latin jazz spilling out of colorful storefronts.

The Sights in a Day

☀️ Start the day off with a freshly squeezed tropical juice with a side of local gossip at **Los Pinareños Frutería** (p97). Get a quick history lesson while visiting the sobering **Cuban Memorial Park** (p95), then check out fast-paced, wise-cracking domino games at **Máximo Gómez Park** (p95).

🌤️ Have lunch at **Versailles** (p96), a long-running favorite of Cuban expats (you'll need to take a bus or car there). Afterwards, head back to the center of Little Havana (pictured left) for browsing souvenirs, *guayaberas* (Cuban dress shirts) and cigars at colorful Calle Ocho shops like **Guantanamera** (p98). Pop by **Cubaocho** (p98) to find out about upcoming concerts and art exhibitions.

🌙 In the evening, grab an early dinner at the secret restaurant spot (it's inside a grocery store) of **El Nuevo Siglo** (p96). Then end the night over mojitos and a bit of live music (if your timing is right) at **Ball & Chain** (pictured left; p97) – a reliable nightspot for a fun evening out. Alternatively catch a taxi out to **Hoy Como Ayer** (p98) for a serious night of salsa.

 Best of Miami

Eating
Versailles (p96)

Doce Provisions (p97)

Drinking & Nightlife
Ball & Chain (p97)

Cubaocho (p98)

Hoy Como Ayer (p98)

Shopping
Little Havana Visitors Center (p98)

Getting There

🚌 **Bus** Bus 8 from Brickell Station makes the 15-minute journey out to Little Havana every 10 to 20 minutes. Note that it travels westbound on 7th St and eastbound (back towards Downtown) on 8th St.

🚲 **Bike** There is one handy Citi Bike station here at SW 8th St and 10th Ave.

SW 11th Ave

SW 11th St

SW 10th St

SW 9th St

7 ✕ ⊗ ▶

SW 8th St (Calle Ocho)

90 41

90 41

968

SW 12th Ave

9 ✕ ⊗

SW 12th Ave

933

6 ⊗ ✕

SW 12th Ct

SW 13th Ave

SW 4th St

SW 5th St

SW 6th St

SW 7th St

SW 8th St (Calle Ocho)

5 ✕

⚐ 2

Cuban Memorial Blvd

Cuban Memorial Park

SW 13th Ct

11 🚇

SW 14th Ave

W Flagler St

SW Flagler Tce

SW 1st St

SW 2nd St

SW 3rd St

SW 14th Ave

12 🚇 14 16

🚇 🚇

SW 14th Ave

Máximo ⚐ 1 Gómez Park

SW 15th Ave

10 8 ⊗ ✕

SW 15th Ave

15 🚇

SW 16th Ave

SW 9th St

SW 10th St

CORAL WAY

SW 16th Ave

SW 17th Ave

SW 17th St

SW 17th Ct

LITTLE HAVANA

4 ⊗ ✕

Little Havana Art District

SW 11th St

SW 11th Tce

SW 12th St

SW 13th St

SW 18th Ave

SW 18th Ave

SW 7th St

SW 8th St (Calle Ocho)

SW 19th Ave

W Flagler St

SW 1st St

SW 3rd St

SW 4th St

SW 5th St

SW 6th St

SW 19th Ave

SW 11th St

SW 12th St

SW 13th St

SW 21st Ave

SW 9th St

SW 21st Ave

SW 22nd Ave

3 ⊗ ✕

13 ⚐

SW 22nd Ave

SW 10th Street Rd

SW 10th St

SW 12th St

500 m

0.25 miles

N

FOTOLUMINATE LLC/SHUTTERSTOCK ©

Men playing dominos in Máximo Gómez Park

Sights

Máximo Gómez Park

PARK

1  Map p94, D3

Little Havana's most evocative reminder of Old Cuba is Máximo Gómez Park, or 'Domino Park,' where the sound of elderly men trash-talking over games of chess is harmonized with the quick clack-clack of slapping dominoes. The jarring backtrack, plus the heavy smell of cigars and a sunrise-bright mural of the 1994 Summit of the Americas, combine to make Máximo Gómez one of the most sensory sites in Miami (although it is admittedly one of the most tourist-heavy ones as well). (cnr SW 8th St & SW 15th Ave; ⊙9am-6pm)

Cuban Memorial Park

MONUMENT

2  Map p94, D3

Stretching along SW 13th Ave just south of Calle Ocho (SW 8th St), Cuban Memorial Park contains a series of monuments to Cuban and Cuban American icons. The memorials include the **Eternal Torch in Honor of the 2506th Brigade**, for the exiles who died during the Bay of Pigs Invasion; a **José Martí memorial**; and a **Madonna statue**, supposedly illuminated by a shaft of holy light every afternoon. (SW 13th Ave, btwn 8th & 11th Sts)

Eating

Versailles
CUBAN $

3   Map p94, A3

Versailles (ver-*sigh*-yay) is an in-stitution – one of the mainstays of Miami's Cuban gastronomic scene. Try the excellent black-bean soup or the fried yucca before moving onto heartier meat and seafood plates. Older Cubans and Miami's Latin political elite still love coming here, so you've got a real chance to rub elbows with Miami's most prominent Latin citizens. (☎305-444-0240; www.versaillesrestaurant.com; 3555 SW 8th St; mains $6-21; ☉8am-1am Mon-Thu, to 2:30am Fri & Sat, 9am-1am Sun)

Lung Yai Thai Tapas
THAI $

4   Map p94, C3

A sure sign of the changing times is this tiny gem in Little Havana, whipping up some truly mouthwatering Thai cooking. Chef Bas performs culinary wizardry with a menu ideal for sharing. You can't go wrong – whether it's perfectly spiced fried chicken wings, tender duck salad or a much-revered Kaho Soi Gai (a rich noodle curry). (☎786-334-6262; 1731 SW 8th St; mains $10-15; ☉noon-3pm & 5pm-midnight)

El Nuevo Siglo
LATIN AMERICAN $

5   Map p94, D3

Hidden inside a supermarket of the same name, the El Nuevo Siglo restaurant draws foodie-minded locals who come for delicious cooking at excellent prices – never mind the unfussy ambience. Grab a seat at the shiny black countertop and nibble on roast meats, fried yucca, tangy Cuban sandwiches, grilled snapper with rice, beans and plantains, and other daily specials. (1305 SW 8th St; mains $8-12; ☉7am-8pm)

Viva Mexico
MEXICAN $

6   Map p94, E2

Head up busy 12th Ave for some of the best tacos in Little Havana. From a take-out window, smiling Latin ladies dole out heavenly tacos topped with steak, tripe, sausage and other meats. There are a few outdoor tables if you want to eat there, but if they're occupied, get it to go. (☎786-350-6360; 502 SW 12th Ave; tacos $2; ☉11am-9pm Tue-Thu, to 11pm Fri & Sat, to 6pm Sun)

 Local Life
Iconic Cinema
Although most people don't go to Little Havana to watch a movie, there's much to recommend the **Tower Theater** (Map p94, D3; ☎305-237-2463; www.towertheatermiami.com; 1508 SW 8th St). This elegant 1920s movie house has a fine deco facade and screens thought-provoking indie and avant-garde fare – with English films subtitled in Spanish. It's a major icon for the neighborhood.

San Pocho
COLOMBIAN $

7 Map p94, E3

For a quick journey to Colombia, head to friendly, always hopping San Pocho. The meat-centric menu features hearty platters like *bandeja paisa* (with grilled steak, rice, beans, fried plantains, an egg, an *arepa* and fried pork skin). There's also *mondongo* (tripe soup) as well as Colombian-style tamales and requisite sides like *arepas* (corn cakes). (☏305-854-5954; www.sanpocho.com; 901 SW 8th St; mains $9-15; ⏱7am-8pm Mon-Thu, to 9pm Fri-Sun)

Azucar
ICE CREAM $

8 Map p94, D3

One of Little Havana's most recognizable snack spots (thanks to the giant ice-cream cone on the facade) serves delicious ice cream just like *abuela* (grandmother) used to make. Deciding isn't easy with dozens of tempting flavors, including rum raisin, dulce de leche, guava, mango, cinnamon, jackfruit and lemon basil. (☏305-381-0369; www.azucaricecream.com; 1503 SW 8th St; ice cream $4-6; ⏱11am-9pm Mon-Wed, to 11pm Thu-Sat, to 10pm Sun)

Doce Provisions
MODERN AMERICAN $$

9 Map p94, E2

For a break from old-school Latin eateries, stop in at Doce Provisions, which has more of a Wynwood vibe than a Little Havana one. The stylish industrial interior sets the stage for dining on creative American fare – rock shrimp mac 'n' cheese, fried chicken with sweet plantain waffle, short-rib burgers and truffle fries – plus local microbrews. (☏786-452-0161; www.doceprovisions.com; 541 SW 12th Ave; mains $11-25; ⏱noon-3:30pm & 5-10pm Mon-Thu, noon-3:30pm & 5-11pm Fri, noon-11pm Sat, 11am-9pm Sun)

Drinking

Ball & Chain
BAR

10 Map p94, C3

The Ball & Chain has survived several incarnations over the years. Back in 1935, when 8th St was more Jewish than Latino, it was the sort of jazz joint Billie Holiday would croon in. That iteration closed in 1957, but the new Ball & Chain is still dedicated to music and good times – specifically, Latin music and tropical cocktails. (www.ballandchainmiami.com; 1513 SW 8th Street; ⏱noon-midnight Mon-Wed, to 3am Thu-Sat, 2-10pm Sun)

Los Pinareños Frutería
JUICE BAR

11 Map p94, D3

Nothing says refreshment on a sultry Miami afternoon like a cool glass of fresh juice (or smoothie) at this popular fruit and veggie stand. Try a combination like the 'abuelo' (sugarcane juice, pineapple and lemon) for something particularly satisfying. The produce is also quite flavorful. (1334 SW 8th St; snacks & drinks $3-6; ⏱7am-6pm Mon-Sat, to 3pm Sun)

Entertainment

Cubaocho

LIVE PERFORMANCE

12 Map p94, D3

Jewel of the Little Havana Art District, Cubaocho is renowned for its concerts, with excellent bands from across the Spanish-speaking world. It's also a community center, art gallery and research outpost for all things Cuban. The interior resembles an old Havana cigar bar, yet the walls are decked out in artwork that references both the classical past of Cuban art and its avant-garde future. (☎305-285-5880; www.cubaocho.com; 1465 SW 8th St; ☺11am-10pm Tue-Thu, to 3am Fri & Sat)

Hoy Como Ayer

LIVE MUSIC

13 Map p94, A3

This Cuban hot spot – with authentic music, unstylish wood paneling and a small dance floor – is enhanced by first-rate mojitos and Havana transplants. Stop in nightly for *son* (a salsalike dance that originated in Oriente, Cuba), *boleros* (a Spanish dance in triple meter) and modern Cuban beats. (☎305-541-2631; www.hoycomoayer. us; 2212 SW 8th St; ☺8:30pm-4am Thu-Sat)

Shopping

Guantanamera

CIGARS

14 Map p94, D3

In a central location in Little Havana, Guantanamera sells high-quality hand-rolled cigars, plus strong Cuban coffee. It's an atmospheric shop, where you can stop for a smoke, a drink (there's a bar here) and some friendly banter. There's also some great live music here most nights of the week. The rocking chairs in front are a fine perch for people-watching if that's your kind of thing. (www. guantanameracigars.com; 1465 SW 8th St; ☺10:30am-8pm Sun-Thu, to midnight Fri & Sat)

Little Havana Visitors Center

GIFTS & SOUVENIRS

15 Map p94, C3

One of the best places in Little Havana to browse for gift ideas. You'll find beautiful (but riotously colorful) Hawaiian-style button-down shirts, Panama hats, eye-catching T-shirts and plenty of kitschy memorabilia (fridge magnets, coffee cups, Cuban-flag bottle openers, etc). They also often offer a taste of Cuban coffee. (1610 SW 8th St; ☺10am-5pm Mon-Sat, to 4pm Sun)

Havana Collection

CLOTHING

16 Map p94, D3

One of the best and most striking collections of the classic traditional *guayaberas* (Cuban dress shirts) in Miami can be found in this shop. Prices are high (plan on spending about $85 for shirt), but so is the quality, so you can be assured of a long-lasting product. (☎786-717-7474; 1421 SW 8th St; ☺10am-6pm)

Understand

Northern Capital of the Latin World

Miami may technically be part of the USA, but it's widely touted as the 'capital of the Americas' and the 'center of the New World.' That's a coup when it comes to marketing Miami to the rest of the world, and especially to the USA, where Latinos are now the largest minority.

A Latin Migration

Miami's pan-Latin mixture makes it more ethnically diverse than any Latin American city. At the turn of the 21st century, the western suburbs of Hialeah Gardens and Hialeah were numbers one and two of US areas where Spanish is spoken as a first language (more than 90% of the population).

How did this happen? Many of Miami's Latinos arrived in this geographically convenient city as political refugees – Cubans fleeing Castro from around the '60s, Venezuelans fleeing President Hugo Chávez, Brazilians and Argentines running from economic woes, Mexicans and Guatemalans arriving to find work.

Latin American Business in Miami

This has all led to the growth of Latin American businesses in Miami, which has boosted the local economy. Miami is the US headquarters of many Latin companies, including Telemundo, one of the biggest Spanish-language broadcasters in the US, as well as MTV Networks Latin America and the Latin branch of the Universal Music Group.

Cuban Americans & Politics

Cubans have a strong influence on local and international politics in Miami. Conservative exile groups have often been characterized as extreme, many refusing to visit Cuba while the Castro family remained in power. While there is still plenty of resentment among older Cubans, the newer generation – often referred to as the 'YUCAs' (Young Urban Cuban Americans) – are more willing to see both sides of issues in Cuba.

The Latino Influence

Whether you're dining out, listening to live music, overhearing Spanish conversations, visiting Little Havana or Little Buenos Aires, or simply sipping a chilled mojito at the edge of your hotel pool, the Latin American energy is palpable, beautiful and everywhere you go.

Explore

Coconut Grove

Coconut Grove was once a hippie colony, but these days its demographic is more middle class. It's a pleasant place to explore with intriguing shops and cafes, and a walkable village-like vibe. It's particularly appealing in the evenings, when residents fill the outdoor tables of its bars and restaurants. Coconut Grove backs onto the waterfront, with a pretty marina and pleasant green spaces.

The Sights in a Day

☼ Beat the crowds by getting an early start at **Vizcaya Museum & Gardens** (p102) – home to one of Miami's most beautiful buildings. Take a leisurely stroll in the serene grounds overlooking the waterfront. Afterwards, head to the center of Coconut Grove for a late breakfast at the excellent **GreenStreet Cafe** (p110).

☼ Burn off those blueberry pancakes on a stroll around the gardens at **Kampong** (p107). You'll have to reserve ahead, but it's well worth the effort to see these beautifully landscaped grounds. Afterwards, check out indie shops like the **Polished Coconut** (p111) and peruse the stores at **CocoWalk** (p111). Save lunch though for the **Spillover** (p109), an atmospheric spot for thoughtfully sourced bistro grub.

☾ Around sunset, perch yourself on the waterside deck of **Monty's Raw Bar** (p109). Come for happy-hour specials, like $1 oysters, and stick around to see the place come to life as regulars hobnob over drinks. Afterwards, have dinner at **Boho** (p109), a great spot to sample Grove cooking at its most creative.

For a local's day in Coconut Grove, see p104.

 Top Sight

Vizcaya Museum & Gardens (p102)

 Local Life

Wandering the Grove (p104)

 Best of Miami

Eating
Spillover (p109)

GreenStreet Cafe (p110)

Boho (p109)

Drinking
Taurus (p110)

Tavern in the Grove (p111)

Shopping
CocoWalk (p111)

Polished Coconut (p111)

Getting There

🚌 **Bus** No 48 takes you from Brickell Ave at SE 14th St (a short walk from the Financial District Metromover station) to the heart of Coconut Grove, traveling along S Bayshore Dr.

🚲 **Bike** There are several Citi Bike kiosks in Coconut Grove, meaning you could cycle here from other parts of the city, particularly Downtown, which is about 5 miles away.

Top Sights
Vizcaya Museum & Gardens

They call Miami the Magic City, and if it is, this Italian villa, the housing equivalent of a Fabergé egg, is its most fairy-tale residence. Perched over the water, Vizcaya is a fascinating place to wander, with art-filled rooms, lavish antique furniture and picturesque gardens.

Map p106, E1

305-250-9133

www.vizcayamuseum.org

3251 S Miami Ave

adult/6-12yr/student & senior $18/6/12

9:30am-4:30pm Wed-Mon

Background

In the early 1900s, the millionaire industrialist James Deering began wintering in South Florida. The Chicago-based bachelor was diagnosed with 'pernicious anemia', for which doctors recommended he spend more time in a warm, sunny climate. And so, in 1912 he bought 130 acres on the edge of Biscayne Bay and began building a grand mansion that took a decade to complete. The work required a staggering amount of manpower with more than 1000 workers taking part in the construction.

The House

The Renaissance-inspired mansion is a classic of Miami's Mediterranean Revival stye. Thirty-four of its original 70 rooms are packed with exquisite artwork and beautifully made furnishings, some of which date back to the 15th century. There's much to gawk at here, from finely painted frescoes to lush stained-glass doors. Deering collected objects not only for their age and beauty, but for the connection to historical figures and events, which adds to the appeal of the collection.

The largest room in the house is the informal living room, dubbed 'the Renaissance Hall' for its works dating from the 14th to 17th centuries. The Admiral Carpet here was created for the grandfather of King Ferdinand of Spain in the 1400s.

The Gardens

On the south side of the house stretches a series of gardens that are just as impressive as the interior of Vizcaya. Modeled on formal Italian gardens of the 17th and 18th centuries, these manicured spaces form a counterpoint to the wild mangroves beyond. Sculptures, fountains and vine-draped surfaces give an antiquarian look to the grounds, and an elevated terrace (the Garden Mound) provides a fine vantage point over the greenery.

☑ Top Tips

▶ Once a month Vizcaya hosts 'Gardens by Moonlight', featuring live music, guided tours through the gardens and a performance by a different artist.

▶ Go early in the day or in the afternoon to capture the best light for taking pictures.

▶ For more insight into Vizcaya, hire the audio guide ($5), which has 90 minutes of content covering background about the house, the gardens and James Deering.

✗ Take a Break

The **Vizcaya Cafe** has made-to-order fare, including salads, empanadas, mahimahi sandwiches and burgers. There aren't other any nearby restaurants, though if you have a car, **El Carajo** (☎ 305-856-2424; www.el-carajo. com; 2465 SW 17th Avenue; tapas $5-15; ☻noon-10pm Mon-Wed, to 11pm Thu-Sat, 11am-10pm Sun; 🚗), located 1 mile northwest, is a magical spot for a meal.

Local Life
Wandering the Grove

Tree-lined streets, outdoor cafes and pretty waterfront green spaces give Coconut Grove a village-like vibe. Its compact center is more walkable than many other parts of Miami, which is a big draw for many residents. Grove folk would agree: strolling among its one-of-a-kind boutiques and neighborhood watering holes is one of the best ways to spend a sunny afternoon.

① Peacock Park

Along the waterfront, this **park** (2820 McFarlane Rd) serves as the great open backyard of Coconut Grove. Families stop by the playground, visitors join the action on the ball fields, while power walkers take in the view on a scenic stroll along the bayfront.

② Glass & Vine

On the edge of Peacock Park, the star attraction of this **eatery** (Map p106, C3;

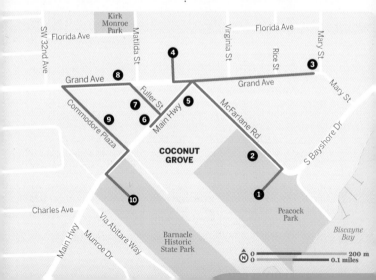

www.glassandvine.com; 2820 McFarlane Rd; mains lunch $9-14, dinner $17-32; ⏱11:30am-3:30pm & 5:30-10pm Sun-Thu, to 11pm Fri & Sat) is its outdoor setting. Offerings at lunch include tabbouleh and shrimp sandwiches; for dinner, try the charred cauliflower and sea scallops.

❸ Book Browsing & Dining

Independent **Bookstore in the Grove** (☎305-483-2855; www.thebookstoreinthe-grove.com; 3390 Mary St; ⏱7am-8pm Mon-Thu, to 9pm Fri & Sat, 8am-8pm Sun) is a good spot for all kinds of lit, and has a great cafe (including all-day breakfast), and even happy-hour drink specials.

❹ First Flight Out

Inside the CocoWalk shopping gallery, this **store** (3015 Grand Ave; www.thefirstflightout.com ⏱11am-10pm Mon-Thu, to 11pm Fri-Sun) sells vintage Pan Am gear – leather satchels, luggage tags, T-shirts and passport covers with that iconic logo from a bygone era of travel.

❺ Panther Coffee

Miami's best coffee purveyor (head-quartered in Wynwood) serves boldly flavored pick-me-ups, plus heavenly bakery items. It's a great **spot** (3407 Main Hwy; www.panthercoffee.com; ⏱7am-9pm Mon-Sat, from 8am Sun; coffees $3-6) to linger over the paper and relax.

❻ Celestial Treasures

Your one-stop **shop** (☎305-461-2341; 3444 Main Hwy; ⏱11am-8pm Sun-Thu, to 10pm Fri & Sat) for spiritual and metaphysical needs, it has books, cards and compo-nents for those interested in Zen,

Buddhism, Hinduism, Wicca, kabbalah and yoga. Also has staff psychics.

❼ Barracuda

Coconut Grove has its share of divey, pretension-free bars, and **Barracuda** (☎305-918-9013; 3035 Fuller St; ⏱noon-3am Tue-Sun, from 6pm Mon) is one of the best of the bunch, with a fine jukebox, pool table, darts and sports on TV. It's a fine retreat from CG's shiny shopping surfaces – it's decorated with wood sal-vaged from an old Florida shrimp boat.

❽ Last Carrot

Going strong since the 1970s, **Last Carrot** (☎305-445-0805; 3133 Grand Ave; ⏱10:30am-6pm Mon-Sat, 11am-4:30pm Sun; mains $6-8) serves up fresh juices, pita sandwiches, avocado melts, veggie burgers and rather famous spinach pies, all amid old-Grove neighborliness.

❾ Bianco Gelato

A much-loved spot in the neighbor-hood, particularly among its youngest residents, **Bianco** (☎786-717-5315; 3137 Commodore Plaza; ice cream $3.50-7) whips up amazing gelato. It's made from or-ganic milk and all natural ingredients.

❿ Barnacle Historic State Park

This 1891, five-acre pioneer residence of Ralph Monroe, Miami's first honorable snowbird is open for guided tours, as is the surrounding **park** (☎305-442-6866; www.floridastateparks.org/thebarnacle; 3485 Main Hwy; admission $2, house tours adult/child $3/1; ⏱9am-5pm Fri-Mon; 👫), which is a shady oasis for strolling. Barnacle hosts moonlight concerts too.

Dinner Key Marina

Vizcaya Museum & Gardens

S Miami Ave

Charthouse Dr

Darwin St

Pan American Dr

Tiger Tail Ave

SW 27th Ave

S Bayshore Dr

Biscayne Bay

Center St

Mary St

Day Ave

Florida Ave

Rice St

Grand Ave

Virginia St

2 Coconut Grove Library

Eva Munroe's Grave

Peacock Park

McFarlane Rd

11

7

Orange St

Oak Ave

COCONUT GROVE

19

Matilda St

Kirk Munroe Park

Barnacle Historic State Park

Via Abitare Way

Munroe Dr

14

Fuller St

16

8

10

Gifford La

Gifford La

Florida Ave

12

Franklin Ave

Commodore Plaza

13

McDonald St

SW 32nd Ave

6

15

Indiana St

Margaret St

Grand Ave

Thomas Ave

William Ave

Charles Ave

Franklin Ave

Main Hwy

Royal Rd

Ohio St

Ohio St

Percival Ave

Oak Ave

Frow Ave

Florida Ave

Plymouth Congregational Church

4

1

For reviews see

◉	Top Sights	p102
◉	Sights	p107
✕	Eating	p108
♥	Drinking	p110
✿	Entertainment	p111
🏠	Shopping	p111

0   400 m
0   0.2 miles

PISAPHOTOGRAPHY/SHUTTERSTOCK ©

Ermita De La Caridad (p108)

Sights

Kampong   GARDENS

1  Map p106, A4

David Fairchild, the Indiana Jones of
the botanical world and founder of
Fairchild Tropical Garden, would rest
at the Kampong (Malay/Indonesian
for 'village') in between journeys in
search of beautiful and economically
viable plant life. Today this lush garden is listed on the National Register
of Historic Places and the lovely
grounds serve as a classroom for the
National Tropical Botanical Garden.
Self-guided tours (allow at least an
hour) are available by appointment, as
are $20 one-hour guided tours. (📞 305-
442-7169; www.ntbg.org/tours/kampong;
4013 Douglas Rd; adult/child $15/5; ⊙ tours
by appointment only 10am-3pm Mon-Sat)

Coconut
Grove Library   HISTORIC BUILDING

2  Map p106, C3

Completed in 1963, the library has
a photogenic design with oolitic
limestone walls and a steep roof
that pays homage to the original
1901 library that stood here. Inside,
there's a small but well-curated refer-
ence section on South Florida. (2875
McFarlane Rd; ⊙ 10am-6pm Mon, Wed, Thu
& Sat, to 8pm Tue, closed Fri & Sun)

Eva Munroe's Grave HISTORIC SITE

 3 Map p106, C3

Tucked into a small gated area near the Coconut Grove Library, you'll find the humble headstone of one Ms Eva Amelia Hewitt Munroe. Eva, who was born in New Jersey in 1856 and died in Miami in 1882, lies in the oldest American grave in Miami-Dade County (a sad addendum: local African American settlers died before Eva, but their deaths were never officially recorded).

Eva's husband Ralph entered a deep depression, which he tried to alleviate by building the Barnacle, now one of the oldest historic homes in the area. (2875 McFarlane Rd)

Plymouth Congregational Church CHURCH

4 Map p106, A4

This 1917 coral church is striking, from its solid masonry to a

 Top Tip

Biking the Grove

If you don't have a car, Citi Bike can be a fine way to get between Coconut Grove and the standout attraction of Vizcaya Museum & Gardens. Just follow the water side of Bayshore Dr (you'll have to use the sidewalk in parts). Along the way, you can peak at marinas and leafy waterfront parks and detour to the Ermita de la Caridad.

hand-carved door from a Pyrenees monastery, which looks like it should be kicked in by Antonio Banderas carrying a guitar case full of explosives and Salma Hayek on his arm. Architecturally this is one of the finest Spanish Mission–style churches in a city that does not lack for examples of the genre. The church opens rarely, though all are welcome at the organ- and choir-led 10am Sunday service. (☑305-444-6521; www.plymouthmiami.org; 3400 Devon Rd; ☺hours vary; ℗)

Ermita de la Caridad MONUMENT

5 Map p106, E1

The Catholic diocese purchased some of the bayfront land from Deering's Villa Vizcaya estate and built a shrine here for its displaced Cuban parishioners. Symbolizing a beacon, it faces the homeland, exactly 290 miles due south. There is also a mural that depicts Cuban history. Just outside the church is a grassy stretch of waterfront that makes a fine spot for a picnic. (☑305-854-2404; www.ermitadela caridad.org; 3609 S Miami Ave)

Eating

LoKal AMERICAN $

6 Map p106, B3

This little Coconut Grove joint does two things very well: burgers and craft beer. The former come in several variations, all utilizing excellent beef (bar the oat and brown-rice version).

When in doubt, go for the frita, which adds in guava sauce, plus melted gruyere and crispy bacon. (📞305-442-3377; 3190 Commodore Plaza; burgers $14-16; ⏱noon-10pm Sun-Tue, to 11pm Wed-Sat; ❄🚲♿)

Spillover
MODERN AMERICAN $$

7 🍴 Map p106, C2

Tucked down a pedestrian strip near the CocoWalk, the Spillover serves up locally sourced seafood and creative bistro fare in an enticing vintage setting (cast-iron stools and recycled doors around the bar, suspenders-wearing staff, brassy jazz playing overhead). Come for crab cakes, buffalo shrimp tacos, spear-caught fish and chips, or a melt-in-your-mouth lobster Reuben. (📞305-456-5723; www.spillovermiami.com; 2911 Grand Ave; mains $13-25; ⏱11:30am-10pm Sun-Tue, to 11pm Wed-Sat; 📶🚲)

Boho
MEDITERRANEAN $$

8 🍴 Map p106, B3

This Greek-run charmer is helping to lead the culinary renaissance in Coconut Grove, serving up fantastic Mediterranean dishes, including tender marinated octopus, creamy risotto, thin-crust pizzas drizzled with truffle oil and zesty quinoa and beet salads. The setting invites long, leisurely meals with its jungle-like wallpaper, big picture windows and easygoing vibe. (📞305-549-8614; 3433 Main Hwy; mains $19-26, pizzas $12-17; ⏱noon-11pm Mon-Fri, from 10am Sat & Sun)

Monty's Raw Bar
SEAFOOD $$

9 🍴 Map p106, E1

Perched over the water, this breezy laid-back spot on Dinner Key turns out some excellent plates of seafood to beautiful bay views. Although Monty's is famous for stone-crab claws, there's plenty more on offer from fried cracked conch to barbecue ribs. Come at happy hour (4pm to 8pm) for $1 oysters and drink specials. (📞305-856-3992; www.montysrawbar.com; 2550 S Bayshore Dr; mains $13-25; ⏱11:30am-11:30pm Sun-Thu, to 1am Fri & Sat)

Glass & Vine
MODERN AMERICAN $$

10 🍴 Map p106, C3

It's hard to beat the open-air setting of this wine-loving eatery on the edge of Peacock Park. Stop by for tabbouleh and shrimp sandwiches at lunch, or charred cauliflower and sea scallops at dinner. All of which go nicely with the extensive wine and cocktail menu. Excellent weekend brunches too. (www.glassandvine.com; 2820 McFarlane Rd; mains lunch $9-14, dinner $17-32; ⏱11:30am-3:30pm & 5:30-10pm Sun-Thu, to 11pm Fri & Sat)

Bombay Darbar
INDIAN $$

11 🍴 Map p106, C2

Indian food is a rarity in Latin-loving Miami and all the more so in Coconut Grove – which makes Bombay Darbar even more of a culinary gem. Run by a couple from Mumbai, this upscale but friendly place hits all the right notes, with its beautifully executed tandooris and tikkas, best accompanied by piping-hot naan and flavor-bursting samosas. (📞305-444-7272; 2901 Florida Ave; mains $15-23; ⏰noon-3pm Thu-Sun, 6-10pm Wed-Mon, closed Tue; 🍴)

Lulu

MODERN AMERICAN $$

12 🍴 Map p106, B3

Lulu is the Grove's exemplar of using local, organic ingredients in its carefully prepared bistro dishes, all of which are best enjoyed at the outdoor tables. You can make a meal of tasty appetizers like roasted dates, Tuscan hummus or ahi tuna tartare, or go for more filling plates of slow-braised pork tacos and seared diver scallops. (📞305-447-5858; 3105 Commodore Plaza; mains lunch $12-19, dinner $15-29; ⏰11:30am-10:30pm Sun-Thu, to 11:30pm Fri & Sat; 🍴)

GreenStreet Cafe

AMERICAN $$

13 🍴 Map p106, B3

Sidewalk spots don't get more popular (and many say more delicious) than GreenStreet, where the Grove's young and gregarious congregate at sunset. The menu of high-end pub fare ranges from roast vegetable and goat cheese lasagna and mesclun endive salad to blackened mahimahi and braised short ribs with polenta. (📞305-567-0662; www.greenstreetcafe.net; 3468 Main Hwy; mains $15-29; ⏰7:30am-1am Sun-Tue, to 3am Wed-Sat)

Jaguar

LATIN AMERICAN $$

14 🍴 Map p106, B2

The menu spans the Latin world, but really everyone's here for the ceviche 'spoon bar.' The idea: pick from six styles of ceviche (raw, marinated seafood), ranging from tuna with ginger to corvina in lime juice, and pull a culinary version of DIY. It's novel and fun, and the ceviche varieties are outstanding. (📞305-444-0216; www.jaguarhg.com; 3067 Grand Ave; mains lunch $15, dinner $22-33; ⏰11:30am-11pm Mon-Sat, 11am-10pm Sun)

Drinking

Taurus

BAR

15 🍷 Map p106, B3

The oldest bar in Coconut Grove is a cool mix of wood paneling, smoky leather chairs, about 100 beers to choose from and a convivial vibe – as neighborhood bars go in Miami, this is one of the best. (📞305-529-6523; 3540 Main Hwy; ⏰4pm-3am Mon-Fri, from 1pm Sat & Sun)

Local Life

Art & Song

If you're in Miami on the first Saturday of the month, don't miss the Fashion + Art + Music (FAM) Night (from 6pm to 9pm October to April), which brings a burst of energy to Grand Ave and Main Hwy with live music and special events at galleries and stores.

Tavern in the Grove BAR

16 Map p106, B2

To say this sweatbox is popular with University of Miami students is like saying it rains sometimes in England. More of a neighborhood dive on weekdays. (☏305-447-3884; 3416 Main Hwy; ☉3pm-3am Mon-Sat, from noon Sun)

Entertainment

Cinépolis Coconut Grove CINEMA

17 ⭐ Map p106, B2

On the upper floor of the CocoWalk shopping complex, this four-screen cinema takes movie-going to the next level. It has Sony 4K digital projection, very comfy seats, and an excellent concession stage – you can even order beer and wine. The lineup is mostly Hollywood first-runs, though occasional indie and foreign films are screened. (☏305-446-6843; www.cinepolisusa.com/coconut-grove; 3015 Grand Ave)

Shopping

Polished Coconut FASHION & ACCESSORIES

18 🔒 Map p106, B3

Colorful textiles from Central and South America are transformed into lovely accessories and home decor at this eye-catching store in the heart of Coconut Grove. You'll find handbags, satchels, belts, sun hats, pillows,

CocoWalk

bedspreads and table runners made by artisans inspired by traditional indigenous designs. (3444 Main Hwy; ☉11am-6pm Mon-Sat, noon-5pm Sun)

CocoWalk MALL

19 🔒 Map p106, B2

Credited for reviving Coconut Grove during the 1990s, CocoWalk is one of the alfresco malls here that houses ubiquitous chain stores, and is perhaps (inexplicably) among the Grove's biggest tourist drawcards. Though there's nothing particularly exceptional here, it's a well-designed space, with a handful or restaurants with outdoor seating amid palm trees, and a top-floor cinema. (3015 Grand Ave; ☉10am-9pm Sun-Thu, to 11pm Fri & Sat)

Explore

Coral Gables

The lovely city of Coral Gables, filled with Mediterranean-style buildings, feels like a world removed from other parts of Miami. Here you'll find pretty banyan-lined streets, and a walkable village-like center, dotted with shops, cafes and restaurants. The big draws are the striking Biltmore Hotel, a lush tropical garden and one of America's loveliest swimming pools.

The Sights in a Day

☀ Start off the day with excellent coffee and creative breakfast fare at local favorite **Threefold** (p122). Afterwards, spend the morning amid butterflies and tropical scenery at the vast **Fairchild Tropical Garden** (p114).

☀ Around lunchtime head back to downtown Coral Gables for top-notch bistro fare at **Frenchie's Diner** (p122). If the weather is warm, follow lunch with a dip in the **Venetian Pool** (p120), a stunning setting for a bit of downtime in the water. Afterwards, take a stroll along the eye-catching shops lining the Miracle Mile. If you need a pick-me-up, grab a coffee at **Books & Books** (p125).

☾ Around sunset, make your way over to the **Biltmore Hotel** (p116), which looks all the grander in the late afternoon South Florida light. It's worth stopping for a snack at the lovely poolside restaurant. That evening, have a dinner of mouthwatering tapas and Spanish Rioja at **Bulla Gastrobar** (p122). Top the night off with a drink at **The Bar** (p124), a nearby watering hole that draws a wide cross-section of Gables society.

 Top Sights

 Best of Miami

Getting There

🚌 **Bus** The free Coral Way trolley travels from Downtown Miami to the heart of Coral Gables at Ponce de Leon Blvd and Coral Way (SW 22nd St).

🚗 **Car** It's a fairly straightforward drive here, with one approach via SW 3rd Ave and on to SW 22nd St. There's ample street parking throughout the Gables, though it's metered (until midnight) nearly everywhere downtown.

Top Sights
Fairchild Tropical Garden

The Fairchild is one of America's most appealing tropical botanical gardens. A butterfly grove, tropical plant conservatory, and gentle vistas of marsh and keys habitats, plus frequent art installations from artists such as Roy Lichtenstein, all contribute to the beauty of this peaceful, 83-acre garden.

Map p119, F5

305-667-1651

www.fairchildgarden.org

10901 Old Cutler Rd

adult/child/senior $25/12/18

9:30am-4:30pm

Creating the Garden

In 1936 the businessman Robert Montgomery founded the botanic gardens. He named it after his friend, the explorer and scientist David Fairchild, who had earned fame for his lifelong travels in search of plants that might be of potential use for the American public. Fairchild donated some of the plants still growing in the garden, including the large African baobab growing by the gatehouse.

Wings of the Tropics

The Wings of the Tropics exhibition is a favorite among young visitors. Inside a gallery, hundreds of butterflies flutter freely through the air, the sheen of their wings glinting in the light. There are some 40 different species represented, including exotics from Central and South America.

One behind-the-scenes highlight is the Vollmer Metamorphosis Lab, where visitors can watch in real time as butterflies emerge from chrysalides. After being nurtured in the lab, they are then released into the Wings of the Tropics exhibit.

Tropical Plant Conservatory

Walking through the Tropical Plant Conservatory and the Rare Plant House feels like stepping back in time. There's much to take in here – rare philodendrons, orchids, begonias, rare palms, rhododendrons, ferns and moss. Plants aside, the other attraction is the oolitic limestone path, which is full of fossils of ancient marine life.

Richard H Simons Rainforest

Though small in size (two acres), this rainforest exhibit provides a taste of the tropics, with a little stream and waterfalls amid orchids, plus towering trees with lianas (long woody vines) and epiphytes up in the rainforest canopy. It was planted in 2000 as a reminder of the incredible biodiversity contained within these endangered forests.

☑ **Top Tips**

▶ Start your visit by taking the 45-minute narrated tram tour. Afterwards, head back to explore in more depth the exhibits that caught your eye.

▶ Time your visit to see daily releases of butterflies in the Wings of the Tropics exhibition. These happen mid-morning and mid-afternoon.

▶ For the most tranquility, go on weekdays when the crowds are thinnest.

✕ **Take a Break**

The onsite Lakeside Café serves sandwiches, salads and desserts in a pretty open-air setting overlooking Pandanus Lake. Alternatively the Glasshouse Café has salads, hot-pressed sandwiches and snacks near the Wings of the Tropics exhibit. Another option is to bring your own picnic and eat on the grounds.

Top Sights
Biltmore Hotel

In the most opulent neighborhood of one of the showiest cities in the world, the Biltmore Hotel has a classic beauty that seems impervious to the passage of years. Its Mediterranean-style architecture, striking interiors and lush tropical grounds can make visitors feel like they've slipped back in time.

👁 Map p118, C4

📞 855-311-6903

www.biltmorehotel.com

1200 Anastasia Ave

🕐 tours 1:30 & 2:30pm Sun

🅿

The Layout

This opulent hotel spreads across 150 acres that encompass tropical grounds, tennis courts, a swimming pool and a 18-hole golf course. You could easily spend a few days never feeling the need to leave the hotel. There's a full-service salon, a plush spa, a 10,000-sq-ft fitness center and a smattering of restaurants – from casual open-air spots to the elegant Palme d'Or. The hotel even has its own intimate theater, with works put on by GableStage.

The Design

The extravagant architecture hits you well before you arrive. There's nothing subtle about the soaring central tower, which was modeled after the 12th-century Giralda tower in Seville, Spain. The grandeur continues on the inside – the colonnaded lobby with its hand-painted ceiling, elaborate antique chandeliers and Corinthian columns, as well as the lushly landscaped courtyard set around a gurgling fountain. The lavish pool is one of the largest in America and resembles a sultan's water garden from *One Thousand & One Nights*.

A Storied Past

The land developer George Merrick who created Coral Gables (also founding the nearby University of Miami) back in the 1920s, joined forces with hotelier John McEntee Bowman to create one of Florida's great hotels of the era. The building, the tallest in Florida at the time, opened to much fanfare in 1926, and quickly became one of the icons of the roaring '20s. President Franklin Roosevelt, the Duke and Duchess of Windsor and Hollywood luminaries including Judy Garland and Bing Crosby were all guests. As were members of the mob from time to time. Al Capone came, as did Thomas 'Fatty' Walsh, who was gunned down by another gangster on the 13th floor. Some say his ghost still roams the hallways.

☑ **Top Tips**

▶ The hotel gives free 45-minute guided tours of the property on Sundays at 1:30pm and 2:30pm.

▶ Visitors can swim in the pool and use the fitness center by purchasing a $35 day pass.

▶ Plan your visit in the morning or afternoon, when the facade seems to glow with a golden light.

▶ Book theater tickets online through www.gablestage.org.

✕ **Take a Break**

Grab lunch or happy-hour drinks at one of the open-air tables of the **Cascade Poolside Restaurant** (mains $15-22; ⏱11:30am-9pm Mon-Fri, from 8am Sat & Sun; 🍴). For something slightly fancier, you can dine on Italian fare at the courtyard restaurant of **Fontana** (mains lunch $16-33, dinner $22-42; ⏱7:30am-3pm & 5-10:30pm Mon-Sat, 7am-10am & 6-10:30pm Sun).

A · B · C · D

1 · 2 · 3 · 4 · 5

SW 57th Ave (Red Rd)

Country Club Prado

N Greenway Dr

Granada Golf Course

S Greenway Dr

Asturia Ave

Castile Ave

Granada Blvd

15

CORAL GABLES

Merrick House 5

Coral Way

Coral Way

Alhambra Cir

N Greenway Dr

Indian Mound Trail

Cordova St

Andalusia Ave

Toledo St

SW 26th St

Salvadore Park

Valencia Ave

Almeria Ave

Venetian Pool 1

Sevilla Ave

Sevilla Ave

DeSoto Plaza

Catalonia Ave

Coral Gables Congregational Church 4

De Soto Blvd

Palermo Ave

Catalonia Ave

Malaga Ave

Granada Blvd

Toledo St

SW 57th Ave (Red Rd)

San Rafael Ave

Anastasia Ave

Biltmore Hotel

Biltmore Golf Course

Durango St

Alhambra Cir

Alhambra Ct

SW 40th St (Bird Rd)

Granada Blvd

17

2

19

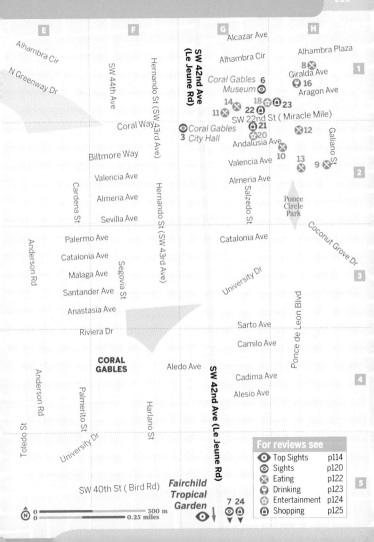

E

Alhambra Cir

N Greenway Dr

F

SW 44th Ave

Hernando St (SW 43rd Ave)

Coral Way

Biltmore Way

Valencia Ave

Almeria Ave

Sevilla Ave

Cardena St

Palermo Ave

Catalonia Ave

Malaga Ave

Santander Ave

Anastasia Ave

Riviera Dr

Anderson Rd

Segovia St

Hernando St (SW 43rd Ave)

G

Alcazar Ave

Alhambra Cir

Coral Gables 6
Museum ◎

14 ✗
11 ✗   18 ◎ 🔒 23
       22 🔒
◎ **Coral Gables** 21 🔒
3 **City Hall**   20
        Andalusia Ave
        10
        Valencia Ave
        13
Almeria Ave

Salzedo St

Catalonia Ave

University Dr

H

Alhambra Plaza

8 ✗
Giralda Ave
🍴 16
Aragon Ave

SW 22nd St (Miracle Mile)

✗ 12

Galiano St

9 ✗ ✗

Ponce
Circle
Park

Coconut Grove Dr

1

2

3

SW 42nd Ave
(Le Jeune Rd)

Ponce de Leon Blvd

Sarto Ave

Camilo Ave

**CORAL
GABLES**

Aledo Ave

SW 42nd Ave (Le Jeune Rd)

Cadima Ave

Alesio Ave

Anderson Rd

Palmerito St

Harlano St

University Dr

Toledo St

SW 40th St (Bird Rd)

*Fairchild
Tropical
Garden*

7 24
◎ ◎
▼ ▼

4

5

◉ N   0   500 m
       0   0.25 miles

For reviews see

◉	Top Sights	p114
◎	Sights	p120
✗	Eating	p122
🍴	Drinking	p123
✿	Entertainment	p124
🔒	Shopping	p125

Sights

Venetian Pool
SWIMMING

1 Map p118, D2

Just imagine: it's 1923, tons of rock have been quarried for one of the most beautiful neighborhoods in Miami, but now an ugly gash sits in the middle of the village. What to do? How about pump the irregular hole full of water, mosaic and tile up the whole affair, and make it look like a Roman emperor's aquatic playground? (☏305-460-5306; www.coralgablesvenetianpool.com; 2701 De Soto Blvd; adult/child Sep-May $15/10, Jun-Aug $20/15; ⏰11am-5:30pm Tue-Fri, 10am-4:30pm Sat & Sun, closed Dec-Feb; ⛹)

Lowe Art Museum
MUSEUM

2 Map p118, D5

Your love of the Lowe, on the campus of the University of Miami, depends on your taste in art. If you're into modern and contemporary works, it's good. If you're into the art and archaeology of cultures from Asia, Africa and the South Pacific, it's great. And if you're into pre-Columbian and Mesoamerican art, it's fantastic. (☏305-284-3535; www.miami.edu/lowe; 1301 Stanford Dr; adult/student/child $13/8/free; ⏰10am-4pm Tue-Sat, noon-4pm Sun)

Coral Gables City Hall
HISTORIC BUILDING

3 Map p118, G2

This grand building has housed boring city-commission meetings since it opened in 1928. It's impressive from any angle, certainly befitting its importance as a central government building. Check out Denman Fink's *Four Seasons* ceiling painting in the tower, as well as his framed, untitled painting of the underwater world on the 2nd-floor landing. (405 Biltmore Way; ⏰8am-5pm Mon-Fri)

Coral Gables Congregational Church
CHURCH

4 Map p118, C3

Developer George Merrick's father was a New England Congregational minister, so perhaps that accounts for him donating the land for the city's first church. Built in 1924 as a replica of a church in Costa Rica, the yellow-walled, red-roofed exterior is as far removed from New England as...well, Miami. The interior is graced with a beautiful sanctuary and the grounds are landscaped with stately palms. (☏305-448-7421; www.gablesucc.org; 3010 De Soto Blvd; ⏰hours vary)

☑ Top Tip

Travel Strategies

The main sights in Coral Gables are out of the town center, and it's not practical to do much exploring without a car. Although you can see some of the highlights in one long day, to make the most of it, consider overnighting in Coral Gables and seeing it all at a more leisurely pace.

Venetian Pool

Merrick House HISTORIC BUILDING

5 ◎ Map p118, D2

It's fun to imagine this simple homestead, with its little hints of Med-style, as the core of what would eventually become the gaudy Gables. When George Merrick's father purchased this plot, site unseen, for $1100, it was all dirt, rock and guavas. The property is now used for meetings and receptions, and you can tour both the house and its pretty organic garden. The modest family residence looks as it did in 1925, outfitted with family photos, furniture and artwork. (☎305-460-5361; 907 Coral Way; adult/child/senior $5/1/3)

Coral Gables Museum MUSEUM

6 ◎ Map p118, G1

This museum is a well-plotted introduction to the oddball narrative of the founding and growth of the City Beautiful (Coral Gables). The collection includes historical artifacts and mementos from succeeding generations in this tight-knit, eccentric little village. The main building is the old Gables police and fire station (note the deco-style firemen faces jutting out of the facade); it's a lovely architectural blend of Gables' Mediterranean Revival and Miami Beach's muscular, Depression-moderne style. (☎305-603-8067; www.coralgablesmuseum. org; 285 Aragon Ave; adult/child/student

$10/3/8; ⊙noon-6pm Tue-Fri, 11am-5pm Sat, noon-5pm Sun)

Matheson Hammock Park PARK

7 Map p118, G5

This 630-acre county park is the city's oldest and one of its most scenic. It offers good swimming for children in an enclosed tidal pool, lots of hungry raccoons, dense mangrove swamps and (pretty rare) alligator-spotting. It's just south of Coral Gables. (☑305-665-5475; www.miamidade.gov/parks/matheson-hammock.asp; 9610 Old Cutler Rd; per car weekday/weekend $5/7; ⊙sunrise-sunset; [P] [♿])

Eating

Threefold CAFE $$

8 Map p118, H1

Coral Gables' most talked-about cafe is a buzzing, Aussie-run charmer that serves up perfectly pulled espressos (and a good flat white), along with creative breakfast and lunch fare. Start the morning with waffles and berry compote, smashed avocado toast topped with feta, or a slow-roasted leg of lamb with fried eggs. (☑305-704-8007; 141 Giralda Ave; mains $13-19; ⊙8am-4:30pm; 🛜 🖊)

Frenchie's Diner FRENCH $$

9 Map p118, H2

Tucked down a side street, it's easy to miss this place. Inside, Frenchie's channels an old-time American diner vibe, with black-and-white checkered floors, a big chalkboard menu, and a smattering of old prints and mirrors on the wall. The cooking, on the other hand, is a showcase for French bistro classics. (☑305-442-4554; www.frenchiesdiner.com; 2618 Galiano St; mains lunch $14-24, dinner $24-34; ⊙11am-3pm & 6-10pm Tue-Sat)

Bulla Gastrobar SPANISH $$

10 Map p118, H2

With a festive crowd chattering away over delicious bites of tapas, this stylish spot has great ambience that evokes the lively eating and drinking dens of Madrid. *Patatas bravas* (spicy potatoes), *huevos* 'bulla' (eggs, serrano ham and truffle oil) and Iberian ham croquettes keep the crowds coming throughout the night. (☑305-441-0107; www.bullagastrobar.com; 2500 Ponce de Leon Blvd; small plates $7-19; ⊙noon-10pm Sun-Thu, to midnight Fri & Sat; 🖊)

Seasons 52 FUSION $$

11 Map p118, G1

It's hard to fault the concept and the execution at Seasons 52. The hook? A menu that partially rotates on a weekly basis depending on what is seasonally available (hence the restaurant's name). The execution? Warm flatbreads overlaid with sharp melted cheese and steak; tiger shrimp tossed in a light pasta and chili that exudes elegance and heartiness all at once. (☑305-442-8552; www.seasons52.com; 321 Miracle Mile; mains $18-31; ⊙11:30am-11pm Mon-Thu, to midnight Fri & Sat, to 10pm Sun; 🖊)

Swine

SOUTHERN US $$$

 12 Map p118, H2

Rustic smoked pork and craft cock-tails come to Coral Gables at this stylish spot near the Miracle Mile. Amid exposed-brick walls, a cascade of hanging light bulbs and reclaimed wood elements, you'd be forgiven for thinking you took a wrong turn on the way to Brooklyn. (786-360-6433; 2415 Ponce de Leon Blvd; mains $20-38, sharing plates $10-25; 10am-10pm Sun-Thu, to midnight Fri & Sat)

Pascal's on Ponce

FRENCH $$$

 13 Map p118, H2

They're fighting the good fight here: sea scallops with beef short rib, crispy duck confit with wild mushroom fricasée and other French fine-dining classics set the stage for a night of high-end feasting. Pascal's is a favorite among Coral Gables food-ies who appreciate time-tested standards. (305-444-2024; www.pascalmiami. com; 2611 Ponce de Leon Blvd; mains lunch $22-31, dinner $31-45; 11:30am-2:30pm Mon-Fri, 6-10pm Mon-Thu, to 11pm Fri & Sat)

Caffe Abbracci

ITALIAN $$$

14 Map p118, G1

Perfect moments in Coral Gables come easy. Here's a simple formula: you, a loved one, a muggy Miami evening, some delicious pasta and a glass of red at a sidewalk table at Abbracci – one of the finest Italian restaurants in the Gables.

Local Life

Japanese Cuisine

Matsuri (Map p118, A5; 305-663-1615; 5759 Bird Rd; mains $12-19, lunch specials $10; 11:30am-2:30pm Tue-Fri, 5:30-10:30pm Tue-Sat), tucked into a nondescript shopping center, is consistently packed with Japanese customers. They don't want scene; they want a taste of home, although many of the din-ers are actually South American Japanese who order *unagi* (eels) in Spanish. Spicy *toro* (fatty tuna) and scallions, grilled mackerel with natural salt, and an ocean of raw fish are all *oishii!* (delicious!)

(305-441-0700; www.caffeabbracci.com; 318 Aragon Ave; mains $19-45; 11:30am-3:30pm Mon-Fri, 6-11pm daily)

Drinking

Seven Seas

BAR

 15 Map p118, A1

Seven Seas is a genuine Miami neigh-borhood dive bar, decorated on the inside like a nautical theme park and filled with numerous University of Miami students, Cuban workers, gays, straights, lesbians and folks from around the way. Come for the best karaoke in Miami on Tuesday, Thursday and Saturday, and for trivia on Monday. (305-266-6071; 2200 SW 57th Ave; noon-1am Sun-Wed, to 2am Thu-Sat)

The Bar
BAR

16 Map p118, H1

All in a name, right? Probably the best watering hole in the Gables, The Bar is just what the title says (which is unusual in this neighborhood of extravagant embellishment). If you're in the 'hood on Friday, come here for happy hour (5pm to 8pm), when young Gables professionals take their ties off and let loose long into the night. (305-442-2730; www.gablesthebar.com; 172 Giralda Ave; 11:30am-3am)

Titanic Brewing Company
MICROBREWERY

17 Map p118, B5

By day Titanic is an all-American-type brewpub, but at night it turns into a popular University of Miami watering hole. Titanic's signature brews are quite refreshing – particularly the White Star IPA. Lots of good pub grub on hand, including Sriracha wings, and corn and crawfish fritters. (305-668-1742; www.titanicbrewery.com; 5813 Ponce de Leon Blvd; 11:30am-1am Sun-Thu, to 2am Fri & Sat)

Entertainment

Coral Gables Art Cinema
CINEMA

18 Map p118, G1

In the epicenter of Coral Gables' downtown, you'll find one of Miami's best art-house cinemas. It screens indie and foreign films in a modern 144-seat screening room. Check out cult favorites shown in the original 35mm format at Saturday midnight screenings (part of the After Hours series). (786-385-9689; www.gablescinema.com; 260 Aragon Ave)

GableStage
THEATER

Founded as the Florida Shakespeare Theatre in 1979 and now housed on the property of the Biltmore Hotel (p116) in Coral Gables, this company still performs an occasional Shakespeare play, but mostly presents contemporary and classical pieces. (305-445-1119; www.gablestage.org; 1200 Anastasia Ave; tickets $48-65)

Cosford Cinema
CINEMA

19 Map p118, D5

On the University of Miami campus, this renovated art house was launched in memory of the *Miami Herald* film critic Bill Cosford. The cinema hosts occasional special events – talks by filmmakers, writers and historians. (305-284-4627; www.cosfordcinema.com; Memorial Classroom Bldg, 5030 Brunson Dr, University of Miami)

Actors Playhouse
THEATER

20 Map p118, G2

Housed within the 1948 deco Miracle Theater in Coral Gables, this three-theater venue stages musicals and comedies, children's theater on its kids stage and more avant-garde productions in its small experimental black-box space. (305-444-9293;

www.actorsplayhouse.org; Miracle Theater, 280 Miracle Mile; tickets $20-64)

Shopping

Bloom   FASHION & ACCESSORIES

 21 Map p118, G2

Bloom is a tiny women's boutique that carries stylish, flattering clothing – perfect for a wardrobe update. Tops with embroideries, colorful maxi dresses, well-made getaway bags and intricately designed jewelry are among the things you'll find. With new arrivals each week, Bloom keeps things fresh. (📞305-476-0300; 290 Miracle Mile; ⊗10:30am-7pm Mon-Thu, to 8pm Fri & Sat)

Retro City Collectibles   MUSIC

22 Map p118, G1

This cluttered little upstairs store is a fun place to browse, with all manner of eye-catching and collectible Americana. You'll find comic books, records, baseball cards, Pez dispensers, old film posters and action figures (Star Wars, Star Trek, Dr Who etc). (📞786-879-4407; 277 Miracle Mile, 2nd fl; ⊗5-9pm Mon-Thu, noon-7pm Sat & Sun)

Books & Books   BOOKS

 23 Map p118, H1

The best indie bookstore in South Florida is a massive emporium of all things literary. B&B hosts frequent readings and is generally just a

Matheson Hammock Park (p122)

fantastic place to hang out; there's also a good restaurant, with dining on a Mediterranean-like terrace fronting the shop. (📞305-442-4408; 265 Aragon Ave; ⊗9am-11pm Sun-Thu, to midnight Fri & Sat)

Village of Merrick Park   MALL

24 Map p118, G5

In upscale Coral Gables, the Village of Merrick Park is a great place to while away a few hours (and not a few dollars). It has dozens of appealing shops, anchored by the classy department stores Neiman Marcus and Nordstrom, plus outdoor restaurants and a cinema. (www.villageofmerrickpark.com; 358 San Lorenzo Ave; ⊗10am-9pm Mon-Sat, noon-6pm Sun)

The Best of
Miami

Miami's Best Walks

Miami's Best...

South Beach art deco district
FOTOSEARCH/GETTY IMAGES ©

Best Walks
Art Deco Architecture

🏃 The Walk

Lovely art deco buildings dot the streets of Miami Beach, transforming this oceanside city into an architectural jewelry box. Ocean Drive is the heart of the historic district, and home to beautifully re-stored hotels, each showcasing its own unique deco style. Along the way be on the lookout for classic Miami motifs: nautical themes (the hotel as cruise liner), tropical imagery (palms, flamingos) and the soft colors meant to evoke the palette of South Florida, from the early light on the water to the soft hues of a winter sunset.

Start Art Deco Museum

Finish The Hotel of South Beach

Length 1.2 miles; two to three hours

🍴 Take a Break

This 'hood is packed with eateries, but Ocean Dr is overpriced. Head over to 11th St Diner for more classic American fare in a 1948 train car instead.

US Post Office

❶ Art Deco Museum

Start at the Art Deco Museum (p32), at the corner of Ocean Dr and 10th St (named Barbara Capitman Way here after the founder of the Miami Design Preservation League). Step in for an exhibit on art-deco style, then head out and go north along Ocean Dr.

❷ The Leslie

Stay on the beach side of Ocean Drive as you walk north for the best views of the buildings. As you stroll, you'll see many fine examples of deco hotels, including the eye-catching Leslie, a boxy shape with eyebrows (cantilevered sun shades) wrapped around the side of the building.

❸ The Cardozo

Cross 13th St and have a look at the **Cardozo** (1300 Ocean Dr), one of the first deco hotels saved by the Miami Design Preservation League. Its beautiful lines and curves evoke a classic automobile from the 1930s.

④ Winter Haven Hotel

Up at 14th St, peek inside the sun-drenched **Winter Haven Hotel** (📞305-531-5571; www.winter havenhotelsobe.com; 1400 Ocean Dr) to see its fabulous floors of terrazzo, made of stone chips set in mortar that is polished when dry. Be sure to look up and check out the deco ceiling lamps, with their sharp, retro sci-fi lines.

⑤ Post Office

Turn down 14th St to Washington Ave and the **US Post Office** (1300 Washington Ave; ⊘8am-5pm Mon-Fri, 8:30am-2pm Sat), at 13th St. Built in Depression Modern style, with a domed cupola and decorative ceiling in the lobby. Note the wall mural depicting a scene of the great Spanish explorer Hernando de Soto encountering/battling Native Americans.

⑥ Wolfsonian-FIU

Walk east to the imposing **Wolfsonian-FIU** (p32), an excellent museum of design, formerly the Washington Storage Company. Wealthy snowbirds of the '30s stashed their pricey belongings here before returning north.

⑦ The Hotel of South Beach

Keep walking along Washington Ave, turn left on 7th St and then continue north along Collins Ave to the The **Hotel of South Beach** (📞305-531-2222; www.the hotelofsouthbeach.com; 801 Collins Ave), featuring an interior and roof deck by Todd Oldham.

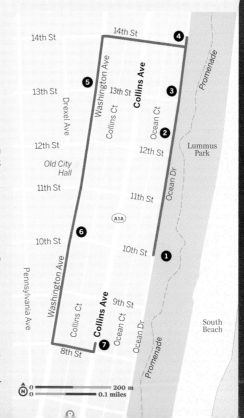

Best Walks
Art & Culture in Wynwood

🏃 The Walk

Wynwood is Miami's unofficial capital of art and all things avant-garde. Its mural lined streets are one giant canvas - albeit one that's ever changing - and its gallery scene is unrivaled. Artwork aside, this dynamic neighborhood harbors many other forms of creativity - from taco stands with secret backroom bars, to empty lots transformed into eating-drinking-concert spaces. Come see it in the daylight, then return by nightfall to see Wynwood at its most vibrant.

Start Art by God Museum Store

Finish Wynwood Brewing Company

Length 1.3 miles; two to three hours

✕ Take a Break

An anchor to the neighborhood, the **Wynwood Yard** (p85) fulfills many roles. Half a dozen food trucks parked here dole out everything from gourmet mac and cheese to healthy vegan bowls.

Panther Coffee

❶ Art by God

Start off at this sprawling **warehouse** (p87) full of matter from the natural world. Triceratops horns, taxidermy of all shapes and sizes and even prehistoric human skulls fill the shelves of this cabinet of curiosity.

❷ Panther Coffee

Walk west to N Miami Ave, take a left, then turn right onto NW 24th St. At the end of the street, you'll run into **Panther Coffee** (p82). Stop at this much-loved coffee roaster for a fine espresso, and take a seat outside for a bit of people watching.

❸ Plant the Future

Turn left and walk up NW 2nd ave to **Plant the Future** (2511 NW 2nd Ave). This tiny shop is a blend of horticulture and sculpture, with small fantastical terrariums, and life-sized creatures sprouting cacti and other greenery.

❹ Wynwood Walls

Across the street is the entrance to the famed **Wynwood Walls** (p74). Take your time wandering through, stopping in the galleries and getting a few good pics among the many brilliant murals before moving on.

❺ Wynwood Building

Exit on 26th St and turn left. Walk up to NW 3rd Ave, and turn right. This takes you through the heart of some truly staggering murals. At the corner of NW27th St is the zebra-striped Wynwood Building, which functions as a creative office and retail space. You'll also find yet another fine coffee spot (Miam Cafe) here.

❻ Margulies Collection at the Warehouse

Exit the building and turn right down 27th St. Two blocks on, you'll reach the **Margulies Collection at the Warehouse** (p80). Although you'll have to pay admission, it's well worth it, as this vast gallery houses an incredible collection of contemporary art.

❼ Wynwood Brewing Company

Turn right when exiting the gallery, walk up to NW 6th St and turn left. Take another left when you reach NW 24th St. In half a block you'll reach the **Wynwood Brewing Company** (p85), one of the pioneers of the microbrew scene in Miami. It has an excellent IPA on tap, as well as a blond ale that goes down easy in steamy Miami.

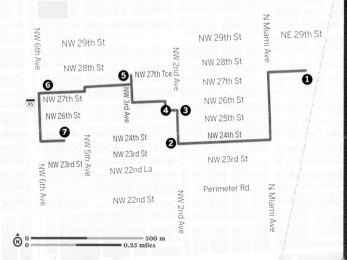

Best
Eating

BONCHAN/SHUTTERSTOCK ©

Miami is a major immigrant entrepôt and a sucker for food trends. Thus you get a good mix of cheap ethnic eateries and high-quality top-end cuisine here, alongside some poor-value dross in touristy zones like Miami Beach. The best new areas for dining are in Downtown, Wynwood and the Upper East Side; Coral Gables has great classic options.

Cuban Cooking

Cuban food, once considered 'exotic,' is itself a mix of Caribbean, African and Latin American influences, and in Miami, it's a staple of everyday life. Sidle up to a Cuban *lonchería* (snack bar) and order a *pan cubano*: a buttered, grilled baguette stuffed with ham, roast pork, cheese, mustard and pickles. In the morning, try a Cuban coffee, also known as café cubano or cortadito. This hot shot of liquid gold is essentially sweetened espresso, while café con leche is just café au lait with a different accent: equal parts coffee and hot milk.

Latin Influences

With its large number of Central and Latin American immigrants, the Miami area offers plenty of authentic ethnic eateries. Seek out Haitian griots (marinated fried pork), Jamaican jerk chicken, Brazilian barbecue, Central American gallo pinto (red beans and rice) and Nicaraguan tres leches ('three milks' cake).

Food Trucks

Food trucks are a huge deal in Miami. You'll find them sprinkled around the city, though a favorite is the Wynwood Yard (p85), which has some excellent options, plus a bar, live music and plenty of outdoor seating. If you're around on the last Friday of the month and have a car, head down to the **Food Truck Invasion** (www.foodtruckinvasion.com) at Tropical Park (7900 SW 40th St), located a few miles southwest of Coral Gables.

Left: *Pan cubano;* Above: Chicken and waffles at Yardbird (p36)

Creative Restaurants

Kyu Creative, flame-kissed cooking in Wynwood. (p83)

27 Restaurant New favorite in Mid-Beach with a globally inspired menu and great atmosphere. (p49)

Yardbird High-end take on Southern cooking. (p36)

El Carajo Delectable tapas served up in a... gas station. (p103)

Best Vegetarian

Chef Allen's Farm-to-Table Dinner Monday night feast by the Arsht Center. (p67)

Dirt Buzzing South Beach cafe with excellent vegetarian choices. (p34)

Manna Life Food Best spot for plant-powered dining Downtown. (p60)

Della Test Kitchen Scrumptious vegan fare at the Wynwood Yard. (p80)

Best Affordable Eats

Coyo Taco Delicious tacos, plus a secret bar in back. (p80)

Cake Thai Rich taste of Thailand, plunked down in Wynwood. (p83)

Kush Perfect combo of burgers and microbrews. (p82)

Wynwood Yard Food trucks, brew and live music. (p85)

Best Latin Cuisine

Yuca Creative takes on Latin American dishes. (p38)

Versailles Long-running Cuban institution near Little Havana. (p96)

El Nuevo Siglo Home-cooked flavors served in a surprising setting. (p96)

CVI.CHE105 Outstanding Peruvian fare in downtown Miami. (p68)

Best
Seafood

Florida has always fed itself from the sea, which lies within arm's reach from nearly every point. If it swims or crawls in the ocean, you can bet some enterprising local has shelled or scaled it, battered it, dropped it in a fryer and put it on a menu.

Fish

Grouper is far and away the most popular fish. Grouper sandwiches are to Florida what the cheese-steak is to Philadelphia or pizza to New York City – a defining, iconic dish, and the standard by which many places are measured. Of course, a huge range of other fish are offered. Other popular species include snapper (with dozens of varieties), mahi-mahi and catfish.

Crustaceans

Florida really shines when it comes to crustaceans: try pink shrimp and rock shrimp, and don't miss soft-shell blue crab – Florida is the only place with blue-crab hatcheries, making them available fresh year-round. Winter (October to April) is the season for Florida spiny lobster and stone crab (out of season, both will be frozen). Florida lobster is all tail, without the large claws of its Maine cousin, and stone crab is heavenly sweet, served steamed with butter or the ubiquitous mustard sauce.

Best Seafood

Joe's Stone Crab Restaurant Legendary seafood purveyor in South Beach. (p37)

Casablanca Fresh-from-the-ocean seafood served on a riverside deck. (p66)

River Oyster Bar Classy, ever popular spot in Brickell. (p67)

SuViche Famed for its tangy ceviche, which goes nicely with pisco-powered cocktails. (p81)

Matsuri Serving up excellent sushi in an unpretentious space much loved by locals. (p123)

Monty's Raw Bar Oysters and other delicacies, plus a laid-back waterside setting. (p109)

Best
Museums

Miami has a treasure chest of great museums. Though the city is best known for its art, there are plenty of other outstanding realms to explore, from science and the biological world to urban design and the legacy of Miami's many immigrant communities.

Pérez Art Museum A beautiful waterfront gallery that stages the top art exhibitions in Miami. (p54)

Wolfsonian-FIU An obligatory stop for anyone interested in 19th and 20th century design. (p32)

The Bass Outstanding collection of European masterpieces in a newly redesigned space. (p34)

HistoryMiami The best place in town to learn about the city's fascinating and complicated history. (p64)

Patricia & Phillip Frost Museum of Science This celebrated new museum downtown has a sprawling collection of interactive exhibits. (pictured above; p64)

Art Deco Museum Small South Beach gem that gives a great overview on Miami's architectural treasures. (p32)

Jewish Museum of Florida-FIU Learn about the deep Jewish ties to Miami's cultural life. (p34)

Coral Gables Museum A quirky museum that celebrates the unique history of a master-planned Mediterranean-inspired village. (p121)

Vizcaya Museum & Gardens Perusing the collection of 18th-century paintings and decorative items feels like stepping into old-world Europe. (p102)

World Erotic Art Museum A fascinating look at eroticism, from ancient sex manuals to Victorian peep-show photos. (p34)

Best
Drinking &
Nightlife

Many people assume Miami's nightlife is all about being wealthy and attractive and/or phony. Disavow yourself of this notion, which only describes a small slice of the scene in South Beach. Miami has an intense variety of bars to pick from that range from grotty dives to beautiful – but still laid-back – lounges and nightclubs.

COURTLAND WHITE/GETTY IMAGES ©

Rooftop Bars

Miami's high rises are put to fine use in the city's many rooftop bars. The big reason to come is of course the view, which can be sublime, with the sweep of Biscayne Bay or sparkling beachfront in the background. If you're here for the panorama and not the scene (DJs, a dressy crowd), come early. Happy hour is fabulous – as you can catch a fine sunset, and getting in is usually not a problem.

Microbreweries & Beer Bars

The microbrew renaissance is underway in Miami with a growing number of craft brewers arriving on the scene. At these Miami spots, you'll find creative brews and a strong neighborhood vibe. Some stock other beers on rotating taps (with a focus on South Florida brewers) as well as their own. Most microbreweries also have food available, or work with food trucks who park outside.

Best Atmosphere

Lagniappe Great bands, excellent provisions and a great backyard, just off the beaten path. (p84)

Broken Shaker A garden of tropical allure (plus fine cocktails and pretty people). (p50)

Sweet Liberty Laid-back local crowd, friendly bar staff and great drinks. (p38)

Mango's Tropical Café Ample amusement at this riotously fun party spot on Ocean Dr. (p38)

The Anderson The perfect neighborhood bar on the Upper East Side. (p89)

Ball & Chain Always a good time at this Little Havana classic. (p97)

AARON DAVIDSON/FILMMAGIC/GETTY IMAGES ©

Blackbird Ordinary (p68)

Best Rooftop Bars

Sugar Swanky spot with a tropical vibe in Brickell. (p61)

Area 31 Join the Happy Hour gang on a Downtown rooftop. (p68)

Eleven Miami Round-the-clock nightclub with a fine terrace. (p68)

Best Beer Bars

Boxelder Friendly neighborhood spot for exploring the South Florida beers. (p86)

Wynwood Brewing Company Pioneer of the microbrew scene in Miami. (p85)

Abbey Brewery The choice spot for a brew in South Beach. (p40)

Best Hidden Gems

Bodega Den of debauchery hidden behind a taco stand. (p38)

Bardot Sultry lounge that's just right for a bit of mischief-making. (p85)

Vagabond Pool Bar Feels like a secret spot. (p89)

Blackbird Ordinary First-rate on all counts: cocktails, music, crowd. (p68)

Best Dive Bars

Kill Your Idol A South Beach watering hole with soul. (p39)

Barracuda A Coconut Grove classic. (p105)

Sandbar Lounge Dig your heels in the sand at this (non-beach) dive. (p50)

Worth a Trip

A Miami icon that's been around since 1979, **Churchill's** (☎ 305-757-1807; www.churchillspub.com; 5501 NE 2nd Ave; ⏰ 3pm-3am Sun-Thu, to 5am Fri & Sat) is a Brit-owned pub in the midst of what could be Port-au-Prince. It's a great spot for a drink, and an even better place to catch live music - indie rock, garage, jazz jams and punk. Just be sure to take a car or taxi there.

Best
Entertainment

Miami's artistic merits are obvious, even from a distance. Could there be a better creative base? There's Southern homegrown talent, migratory snowbirds bringing the funding and attention of northeastern galleries, and immigrants from across the Americas. All that adds up to some great live music, theater and dance – with plenty of room for experimentation.

DAYOWL/SHUTTERSTOCK ©

Film

With such a diverse global audience here, you'll find plenty of intriguing foreign fare, as well as indie films and documentaries. Miami has a glut of art-house cinemas showing these sorts of films as well as plenty of Hollywood features.

Theater

Miami has a small but vibrant theater scene. In addition to small playhouses around town, you can catch big Broadway shows and marquee groups take the stage at the Adrienne Arsht Center for the Performing Arts and other sizable venues. See www.southfloridatheatre.com for a comprehensive directory of playhouses in greater South Florida.

Best Performing Arts Venues

Adrienne Arsht Center for the Performing Arts World-class repertoire of Broadway shows, concerts, opera and ballet. (p56)

Olympia Theater Great venue for all types of shows and concerts. (p70)

Cubaocho Intimate setting for top performers from Latin America and beyond. (p98)

New World Center Miami Beach's iconic concert hall. (p32)

Best Cinemas

Coral Gables Art Cinema Indie and foreign films in a 144-seat cinema. (p124)

Tower Theater In a gem of a deco building, managed by Miami Dade College. (pictured above; p96)

O Cinema Indie screenings in Wynwood. (p86)

Best Theaters

Actors Playhouse A well-loved classic, in the heart of downtown Coral Gables. (p124)

Gablestage Thought-provoking works staged in the Biltmore. (p124)

Light Box at Goldman Warehouse Creative fare at a Wynwood incubator of the arts. (p86)

Best
Music

There's always something happening on the music scene in Miami. You can catch brassy Latin jazz around town (including in Little Havana), hear indie rockers playing in backyard settings around Wynwood, and see bigger name groups take to big arenas and music halls. The city's packed festival calendar is another great opportunity to catch some live music.

GUSTAVO CABALLERO/GETTY IMAGES FOR TIDAL ©

Lagniappe Atmospheric place to catch local bands - either in the backyard or in the vintage indoor bar. (p84)

Gramps A Wynwood classic with a backyard stage for the easy-going beer drinking crowd. (p86)

Churchill's Going strong in Little Haiti since 1979, this place is a must for indie rock fans. (p137)

The Anderson Join the neighborhood crowd for Thursday night jam sessions. (p89)

Ball & Chain A fun place in Little Havana for live music, especially on salsa nights. (p97)

Mango's Tropical Café Salsa lovers pack the dance floor in the back bar as live bands fire up the crowd. (p38)

Fillmore Miami Beach Art-deco venue staging a wide variety of fare. (pictured above; p41)

Hoy Como Ayer A dance-loving spot that draws fiery Latin bands. (p98)

☑ **Music Listings**

Check out listings for upcoming concerts in the Miami New Times (www.miaminewtimes.com/music).

North Beach Bandshell Great place to enjoy outdoor concerts. (p51)

Barnacle Historic State Park Catch outdoor moonlight concerts in this serene waterfront park. (p105)

Best
Festivals &
Events

Art Basel Miami Beach

(www.artbasel.com/miami-beach; ☺early Dec) One of the most important international art shows in the world, this four-day fest has open-air art installations around town, special exhibitions at many galleries and outdoor film screenings among other goings-on.

Wynwood Life (www.

wynwoodlife.com; ☺Apr) A celebration of all things Wynwood, with live music and DJs, a big market of arts and crafts, fashion shows, food trucks, a culinary stage and a crew of talented street artists creating live installations throughout the fest.

Art Deco Weekend

(www.artdecoweekend. com; Ocean Dr, btwn 1st St & 23rd St; ☺mid-Jan) This weekend fair held in mid-January features guided tours, concerts, classic-auto shows, sidewalk cafes, arts and antiques.

Calle Ocho Festival

(Carnaval Miami; www.carnavalmiami.com; ☺Mar) This massive street party in March is the culmination of Carnaval Miami, a 10-day celebration of Latin culture.

Coconut Grove Arts Festival (www.coco

nutgroveartsfest.com; Bayshore Dr, Coconut Grove; ☺late-Feb) This three-day February fair features works by more than 350 visual artists, plus concerts, dance and theater troupes, a culinary arts component and a global village with vendors selling foods from around the world.

Independence Day

Celebration (Bayfront Park; ☺July 4) July 4 is marked with excellent fireworks, a laser show and live music that draw more than 100,000 people to breezy Bayfront Park.

Miami Beach Gay

Pride (www.miamibeach gaypride.com; ☺Apr)

In April, Miami Beach proudly flies the rainbow flag high in this weekend festival that culminates in a colorful street parade along Ocean Dr.

Miami International

Film Festival (www. miamifilmfestival.com; ☺Mar) A 10-day festival showcasing documentaries and features from all over the world. Over half-a-dozen cinemas participate.

Miami Museum Month

(www.miamimuseum month.com; ☺May) Held through the month of May, this is an an excellent chance to hang out in some of the best museums in the city in the midst of happy hours, special exhibitions and lectures.

Best
Shopping

Temptation comes in many forms in Miami. For shoppers, this means high-end fashion, designer sunglasses, vintage clothing, books, records, Latin American crafts, artwork, gourmet goodies, and much more. You'll also find sprawling air-conditioned malls where you can retreat when the weather sours.

JOE RAEDLE/GETTY IMAGES ©

Lincoln Road

Lincoln Road Mall, an outdoor pedestrian thoroughfare between Alton Rd and Washington Ave, is packed with boutiques, galleries and outdoor restaurants. Carl Fisher, the father of Miami Beach, envisioned the road as a Fifth Ave of the South, and it makes a lovely setting for a shopping-minded stroll amid shady overhangs, fountains and greenery.

Fashion & Accessories

Supply & Advise Downtown shop with ruggedly elegant menswear. (p61)

Bloom An essential boutique when strolling the Miracle Mile. (p125)

Havaianas Essential beachwear while in Miami. (p42)

Alchemist Pricey apparel, but fun to browse. (p29)

Nomad Tribe Stylish sustainably sourced apparel, with several locations. (pictured above; p42)

Shinola Beautifully crafted watches and accessories. (p87)

Books

Bookstore in the Grove The perfect neighborhood bookseller. (p105)

Books & Books Atmospheric spot for browsing, with a great cafe. (p42)

Taschen Tiny shop, big beautiful art books. (p29)

Gifts & Souvenirs

Malaquita Ceramics, baskets and unusual wares from Latin America. (p87)

The Bazaar Project Eye-catching curiosities from a small Design District shop. (p77)

Music

Brooklyn Vintage & Vinyl A much-loved new record shop near Wynwood. (p87)

Retro City Collectibles A fine selection of records, plus comic books, film posters and more. (p125)

Best
For Kids

JAMES KIRKIKIS/SHUTTERSTOCK ©

Miami has loads of attractions for young travelers. You'll find lovely beaches, grassy parks, nature trails, megamalls, zoos and other animal-centric attractions. Plus, there's plenty of great snacks, from Italian-style *gelato* to Venezuelan *arepas* (corn cakes). There are also loads of family-friendly hotels and restaurants to keep your young ones happy on holiday.

Beaches & Pools

Venetian Pool Spend the day splashing about in Miami's loveliest swimming pool. (p120)

South Pointe Park Ice-cream stands, soft grass, a beach and mini waterpark. (p36)

Boardwalk Fronts a family-friendly stretch of sand in Mid-Beach. (p48)

Crandon Park Pretty Key Biscayne spot with sand and nature trails. (p91)

Bill Baggs Cape Florida State Park Picnic tables front a pretty sweep of beach, plus scenic walks among the greenery. (pictured above; p91)

Parks & Green Spaces

Bayfront Park Right in Downtown, with open spaces for running around, a good playground and outdoor dining nearby. (p61)

Oleta River State Park Huge park with waterfront access, and canoe and kayak rental. (p48)

Marjory Stoneman Douglas Biscayne Nature Center Aquarium exhibits, short nature trails, and once monthly kid-focused outdoor activities. (p91)

Vizcaya Museum & Gardens Older children will appreciate the whimsy of this fairy-tale mansion and sprawling gardens. (p102)

Barnacle Historic State Park Outdoor paths and frequent family-friendly outdoor concerts. (p105)

Rainy Day Activities

Miami Children's Museum An indoor playland where kids can go on many imaginary adventures (including under the sea). (p65)

HistoryMiami Fascinating multimedia exhibits on Miami's history; there's even displays on pirates! (p64)

Patricia & Phillip Frost Museum of Science Aquarium, planetarium and hands-on exhibits exploring the wonders of the natural world. (p64)

Best
Tours

Miami is a great city for exploring on your own, but for deeper insight, consider signing up for a guided tour. Top guides can shed light on the history, culture and cuisine of Miami, on a wide range of short- or all-day excursions. Highlights include architecture strolls, art-focused walks and food tours, where you get to taste your way around the city.

FID DE/GETTY IMAGES ©

Miami Design Preservation League

(☏305-672-2014; www.mdpl.org; 1001 Ocean Dr; guided tours adult/student $25/20; ☉10:30am daily & 6:30pm Thu) Tells the history behind the art-deco buildings in South Beach, with a lively guide from the Miami Design Preservation League.

Wynwood Art Walk

(☏305-814-9290; www.wynwoodartwalk.com; tours from $29) Not to be confused with the monthly art celebration of the same name, this walk is actually a 90-minute guided tour taking you to some of the best gallery shows of the day, plus a look at some of the top street art around the 'hood.

Miami Food Tours

(☏786-361-0991; www.miamifoodtours.com; 429 Lenox Ave; South Beach tour adult/child $58/35, Wynwood tour $75/55; ☉tours South Beach 11am & 4:30pm daily, Wynwood 10:30am Mon-Sat) Highly rated tour that explores various facets of the city – culture, history, art, and of course cuisine – while making stops at restaurants and cafes along the way.

Miami EcoAdventures

(☏305-666-5885; www.miamidade.gov/ecoadventures; bike tours $45, canoeing $30-70) Offers a variety of tours, including bike tours on Key Biscayne and canoe trips on the Oleta River, plus kayaking, snorkeling, walking and birdwatching.

History Miami Tours

(www.historymiami.org/city-tour; tours $30-60) Historian extraordinaire Dr Paul George leads fascinating walking tours, including culturally rich strolls through Little Haiti, Little Havana, Downtown and Coral Gables at twilight, plus the occasional boat trip to Stiltsville and Key Biscayne.

South Beach Diver & Surf Center

(☏305-531-6110; www.southbeachdivers.com; 850 Washington Ave; 2-tank dive trip without/with gear from $90/140, surfboard hire 4hr/all day $30/35; ☉9am-7pm Mon-Sat, 10am-6pm Sun) Leads regular diving excursions down to the reefs of Key Largo plus night dives, wreck dives and shark dives.

Urban Tour Host

(☏305-416-6868; www.miamiculturaltours.com; 25 SE 2nd Ave, Ste 1048; tours from $20) Runs a program of tours that provide face-to-face interaction in all of Miami's neighborhoods.

Best
Activities

Miami doesn't lack for ways to raise your heart rate. From kayaking pristine waters to hiking through tropical undergrowth, yoga in the parks and (why not?) a somewhat gentle birch-branch beating at a Russian sauna. The Magic City rewards those who want an active holiday.

Bicycling

Some good trails include the Old Cutler Bike Path, which starts at the end of Sunset Dr in Coral Gables and leads through Coconut Grove to Matheson Hammock Park and Fairchild Tropical Garden. The Rickenbacker Causeway takes you up and over the bridge to Key Biscayne for gorgeous water views.

Running

Popular destinations for a run include the Flamingo Park track, located east of Alton Rd between 11th St and 12th St; Promenade in South Beach for its style; the boardwalk on Mid-Beach for great people-watching and scenery; and South Bayshore Dr in Coconut Grove for its shady banyan trees.

Diving & Snorkeling

Head to the Keys or Biscayne National Park. If you don't have a car, dive operators in town lead organized day trips, taking you to colorful coral reefs like the John Pennekamp State Park in Key Largo.

Yoga

The beach is definitely not the only place to salute the sun in Miami. There are lovely yoga studios all across town, and even free classes - like in Bayfront Park. Studios offer a large range of classes; most participants bring their own mat, though many places hire out them out for around $2 a class.

ANOUCHKA/GETTY IMAGES ©

☑ Buying Tickets

With so many teams (pro, college) and special tournaments happening in Miami, there's rarely a sports-free day in this city. Some teams offer tickets directly on their website, but most sell tickets via Ticketmaster (www.ticketmaster.com) or Stubhub (www.stubhub.com).

Yoga on South Beach

Day Spas

As you may have guessed, Miami offers plenty of places to get pampered. Some of the most luxurious spas in town are found at high-end hotels, where you can expect to pay $300 to $400 for a massage and/or acupressure, and $200 for a body wrap.

Virginia Key Beach North Point Park Looking for manatees and bird life on a peaceful paddle off Virginia Key. (p91)

South Beach Taking to the sands for an early-morning sunrise jog along Miami Beach. (p32)

Key Biscayne Hiring a bike for the ride over the causeways and out along Key Biscayne. (p90)

Venetian Pool A lovely spot to splash around. (p120)

Bayfront Park Joining locals in a free outdoor yoga session. (p61)

Oleta River State Park A magical setting for kayaking or canoeing amid the mangroves. (p48)

Marjory Stoneman Douglas Biscayne Nature Center Take to the short nature trails for a look at South Florida's wild side. (p91)

Barnacle Historic State Park Hosts twice weekly evening yoga classes in the lovely outdoor setting. (p105)

Carillon Miami Wellness Resort A truly decadent spa experience (p47)

Russian & Turkish Baths Old-school steam baths plunked straight out of the old country. (p48)

American Airlines Arena Catch the Miami Heat in fast-paced basketball games at this downtown stadium. (p70)

Best
For Free

It's no secret that Miami can quickly put a dent in the travel budget. Luckily, the city offers some excellent free attractions - from behind-the-scenes concert hall tours to some outstanding admission-free art galleries. The star attraction is of course the beach, which is free and open to all.

FELIX MIZIOZNIKOV/SHUTTERSTOCK ©

Wynwood Walls One of Miami's best-loved sights is an ever-changing installation of raw beauty. (p74)

De La Cruz Collection A stunning collection of works - always free to visit - in the Design District. (p77)

Bakehouse Art Complex Cutting-edge works by contemporary artists in Wynwood. (p80)

SoundScape Park Catch free outdoor film screenings throughout the year in South Beach. (p32)

Biltmore Hotel Explore at your leisure the public spaces of this grand dame. Or join a free tour on Sundays (1:30pm and 2:30pm). (p116)

Fly's Eye Dome A geodesic dome and iconic public sculpture tucked away in the Design District. (p77)

Locust Projects Often stages some excellent art exhibitions. (p76)

Adrienne Arsht Center for the Performing Arts Offers free guided tours at noon on Mondays and Saturdays. (pictured above; p56)

Pérez Art Museum Miami Take advantage of free admission days on the first Thursday and the second Saturday of the month. (p54)

Bayfront Park Take a free yoga class, given Mondays and Wednesdays at 6pm and Saturday at 9am. (p61)

Survival Guide

Survival Guide

Before You Go

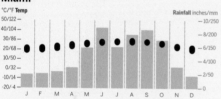

When to Go

Miami

°C/°F Temp

Rainfall inches/mm

50/122 —
40/104 —
30/86 —
20/68 —
10/50 —
0/32 —
-10/14 —
-20/-4 —

— 10/250
— 8/200
— 6/150
— 4/100
— 2/50
— 0

J F M A M J J A S O N D

➡ **Winter (Dec–Feb)**
The warm, dry weather draws in tourists; hotel prices and crowds are at their peak, though it's also the liveliest season with a packed calendar of festivals and big events.

➡ **Spring (Mar–Jun)**
It isn't as muggy as deep summer, but lusher and greener than winter.

➡ **Summer (Jul–Sep)**
It's hot! Prices plummet. When the temperatures aren't sweltering there are storms: it's hurricane season.

➡ **Autumn (Oct–Nov)**
The shoulder season can yield decent prices, while the warm weather ensures ample beach days.

Book Your Stay

Useful Websites

➡ **Greater Miami & the Beaches** (www.miamiandbeaches.com/where-to-stay) Lowdown on great stays in Miami, whether after luxury, architectural beauty or ocean views.

➡ **Miami.com** (www.miami.com/category/miami-hotels-motels) Curated insight into top hotels and new openings.

➡ **Lonely Planet** (www.lonelyplanet.com/usa/miami/hotels) Accommodation reviews and online booking services.

Best Budget

Freehand Miami (www.thefreehand.com) Affordable dorms, stylish private rooms and a beautiful backyard.

SoBe Hostel (www.sobe-hostel.com) Great South Beach location with a friendly crowd and lots of activities.

HI Miami Beach (www.hi-miamibeach.com) Welcoming, easygoing spot in the heart of South Beach.

Rock Hostel (www.miamirockhostel.com) Magnet for nightlife seekers.

Best Midrange

Townhouse Hotel (www.townhousehotel.com) Lively rooftop bar, a hidden burger and ramen joint and an easygoing vibe.

Langford Hotel (www.langfordhotelmiami.com) Classy Downtown option in a Beaux Arts beauty.

Vagabond Hotel (www.thevagabondhotel.com) Restored 1950s beauty, with retro rooms and a lovely pool bar.

Real Living Residence (www.rlmiami.com) Near Wynwood, RLR makes a handsome crash pad while taking in the art scene.

Best Top End

Biltmore Hotel (www.biltmorehotel.com) Gem of Mediterranean Revival style, and amenities galore – including Florida's biggest pool.

Washington Park Hotel (www.wphsouthbeach.com) A hotel spread among five deco buildings with an eye-catching courtyard and a great bar.

Betsy Hotel (www.thebetsyhotel.com) Top South Beach choice for excellent service and amenities.

EAST, Miami (www.east-miami.com) Sweeping views, top amenities and Downtown's best rooftop bar.

Miami Beach Edition (www.editionhotels.com/miami-beach) High-design from Ian Schrager, with a beautiful nightclub and indoor skating rink.

1 Hotel (www.1hotels.com/south-beach) Green credentials, multiple pools, a kids club and rooms that you'll never want to leave.

Arriving in Miami

Miami International Airport

➡ Taxis charge a flat rate, which varies depending on where you're heading. It's $22 to Downtown, Coconut Grove or Coral Gables; $35 to South Beach; and $44 to Key Biscayne. Count on 40 minutes to South Beach in average traffic, and about 25 minutes to Downtown.

➡ Metro buses leave from Miami Airport Station (connected by electric rail to the airport) and run throughout the city; fares are $2.25.

➡ The Miami Beach Airport Express (bus 150) costs $2.65 and makes stops all along Miami Beach, from 41st to the southern tip.

➡ The SuperShuttle shared-van service costs about $22 to South Beach. Be sure to reserve a seat the day before.

Money-Saving Tips

Nearly every bar has happy hour, which typically runs from about 5pm to 7pm Monday through Friday. Most places also have discounted food specials in addition to cheaper drink prices.

➜ Some hotels offer free shuttles.

➜ If you're driving, follow Rte 112 from the airport, then head east on the Julia Tuttle Causeway or the I-195 to get to South Beach.

Fort Lauderdale-Hollywood International Airport

➜ By taxi, count on at least 45 minutes from the airport to Downtown, and at least an hour for the ride to South Beach. Prices are metered. Expect to pay about $65 to Downtown and $75 to South Beach.

➜ Shared-van service is available from the airport with GO Airport Shuttle. Prices are around $25 to South Beach.

➜ Take the free shuttle to the airport's Tri-Rail station. There you can hop aboard this commuter train into Miami ($3.75 to $5), which connects with Miami-Dade's Metrorail Orange Line. Trains run every 30 to 60 minutes, so be mindful of departure times to avoid long waits.

Getting Around

Car

➜ You can find great deals on car rental in Miami, with rates starting as low as $20 per day. It's useful to have a car if you want to do some exploring beyond South Beach and Downtown, particularly for visiting places like Coral Gables and North Miami Beach.

➜ There are car-rental agencies all over town, with loads of options in Miami Beach, in Downtown Miami and at the airport.

➜ You must pay for parking nearly everywhere (though it's generally free from 3am to 9am – from midnight in some places). If you park without paying, you may be towed and have to pay upwards of $200 plus all the associated headaches to retrieve your vehicle.

➜ Most on-street parking is now done by smartphone app or pay by phone (though there are still a few pay-and-display ticket machines at some locations).

The app to use in Miami is Pay By Phone (www.paybyphone.com). In Miami Beach, you'll need to use Park Mobile (www.parkmobile.com).

➜ Parking rates vary, but typically range between $1.50 and $3 per hour. There are many municipal parking garages, which are usually the easiest and cheapest option – look for giant blue 'P' signs. You'll find several located along Collins Ave and Washington Ave.

Taxi & Ride Sharing

➜ For a 20-minute trip (Lincoln Rd to Brickell City Center, for instance), the fare is upwards of $30.

➜ Given the high prices of taxis, and inconvenience of ordering them, most Miami residents use ride-sharing apps such as Lyft and Uber.

➜ Taxis are hard to hail on the street. You'll generally have to call one.

➜ **Central Cabs** (📞 305-532-5555), **Metro** (📞 305-888-8888) and **Miami Taxi Service** (📞 305-525-2455) are several big taxi operators.

Bus

➡ Miami's local bus system is called **Metrobus** (📞 305-891-3131; www.miamidade.gov/transit/routes.asp; tickets $2.25) and, though it has an extensive route system, service can be pretty spotty.

➡ Each bus route has a different schedule and routes generally run from about 5:30am to 11pm, though some are 24 hours.

➡ Rides cost $2.25 and must be paid in exact change (coins or a combination of bills and coins) or with an Easy Card (available for purchase from Metrorail stations and some shops and pharmacies).

➡ An easy-to-read route map is available online. Note that if you have to transfer buses, you'll have if pay the fare each time if paying in cash. With an Easy Card, transfers are free.

Trolleys

➡ A free bus service runs along routes in Miami, Miami Beach, Coconut Grove, Little Havana and Coral Gables, among other locations. The Trolley (www.miamigov. com/trolley) is actually a hybrid-electric bus disguised as an orange and green trolley.

➡ Miami Beach (www.miamibeachfl.gov/transportation) has four trolleys running along different routes, with arrivals every 10 to 15 minutes from 8am to midnight (from 6am Monday to Saturday on some routes).

Bicycle

➡ Miami is flat, but traffic can be horrendous (abundant and fast-moving), and there isn't much biking culture (or respect for bikers) just yet.

➡ **Citi Bike** (📞 305-532-9494; www.citibikemiami.com; 30min/1hr/2hr/4hr/1-day rental $4.50/6.50/10/18/24) is a bike-share program where you can borrow a bike from scores of kiosks spread around Miami and Miami Beach.

➡ Free paper maps of the bike network are available at some kiosks, or you can find one online. There's also a handy iPhone app that shows you where the nearest stations are.

➡ For longer rides, clunky Citi Bikes are not ideal (no helmet, no lock and only three gears). Instead, hire a bike from **Bike & Roll** (📞 305-604-0001; www.bikemiami.com; 210 10th St; hire per 2hr/4hr/day from $10/18/24, tours $40; ⊙9am-7pm) or **Brickell Bikes** (📞 305-373-3633; www.brickellbikes.com; 70 SW 12th St; bike hire 4/8 hours $20/25; ⊙10am-7pm Mon-Fri, to 6pm Sat).

Essential Information

Business Hours

Unless otherwise noted the standard business hours in Miami are as follows:

Banks 8:30am to 4:30pm Monday to Thursday, to 5:30pm Friday; sometimes 9am to 12:30pm Saturday.

Bars In Miami, most bars 5pm to 3am; in Miami Beach, most bars close at 5am.

Businesses 9am to 7pm Monday to Friday.

Restaurants Breakfast 7am to 10:30am Monday to Friday; brunch 9am to 2pm Saturday and Sunday; lunch 11:30am to 2:30pm Monday to Friday; dinner 5pm to 10pm, later Friday and Saturday.

Post Offices 9am to 5pm Monday to Friday; sometimes to noon Saturday.

Shops 10am to 6pm Monday to Saturday, noon to 5pm Sunday; shopping malls keep extended hours.

Electricity

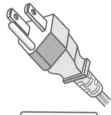

Type B
120V/60Hz

Type A
120V/60Hz

Emergency

Ambulance, Police, Fire
☎911

Money

➡ ATMs are widely available, though most ATM withdrawals using out-of-state cards incur surcharges of $3 or so.

➡ Major credit cards are widely accepted.

Public Holidays

On the following dates, banks, schools and government offices are closed, and transportation, museums and

other services operate on a Sunday schedule. Many stores, however, maintain regular business hours. Holidays falling on a weekend are usually observed the following Monday.

New Year's Day January 1

Martin Luther King Jr Day Third Monday in January

Presidents Day Third Monday in February

Memorial Day Last Monday in May

Independence Day July 4

Labor Day First Monday in September

Columbus Day Second Monday in October

Veterans Day November 11

Thanksgiving Fourth Thursday in November

Christmas Day December 25

Safe Travel

Miami is a fairly safe city, but there are a few areas considered by locals to be dangerous:

➡ Liberty City, in northwest Miami; Overtown, from 14th St to 20th St;

Little Haiti and stretches of the Miami riverfront.

➡ South Beach, particularly along the carnival-like mayhem of Ocean Dr between 8th and 11th Sts, and deserted areas below 5th St can also be dangerous late at night.

➡ Use caution around causeways, bridges and overpasses where homeless people have set up shantytowns.

➡ In these and other reputedly 'bad' areas, you should avoid walking around alone late at night. It's best to take a taxi.

Toilets

You'll find public toilets at some parks and at various posts along city beaches. Outside of this, public toilets can be sparse. It's best to pop into a cafe.

Tourist Information

Greater Miami & the Beaches Convention & Visitors Bureau (☏305-539-3000; www.miamiandbeaches.com; 701 Brickell Ave, 27th fl; ⊙8:30am-6pm Mon-Fri) Offers loads of info on Miami and keeps

up-to-date with the latest events and cultural offerings.

Art Deco Welcome Center (☏305-672-2014; www.mdpl.org; 1001 Ocean Dr, South Beach; ⊙9:30am-5pm Fri-Wed, to 7pm Thu) Run by the **Miami Design Preservation League** ((MDPL); ☏305-672-2014; www.mdpl.org; 1001 Ocean Dr; guided tours adult/student $25/20; ⊙10:30am daily & 6:30pm Thu); has tons of art-deco district information and organizes excellent walking tours.

Downtown Miami Welcome Center (☏305-448-7488; www.downtownmiami.com; 100 NE 1st Ave; ⊙noon-5pm Mon, 10am-5pm Tue-Sat) Provides maps, brochures and tour information for the Downtown area.

Coral Gables Visitor Center (www.coralgables.com; 285 Aragon Ave; ⊙9am-5pm Mon-Fri, 10am-3pm Sat) Set in the Coral Gables Museum, this friendly center has loads of tips on exploring the town.

Travelers with Disabilities

➡ Most public buildings are wheelchair accessible and have appropriate restroom facilities.

➡ Transportation services are generally accessible to all.

➡ Many banks provide ATM instructions in Braille.

➡ Many busy intersections have audible crossing signals and curb ramps are common.

Visas

➡ All visitors should reconfirm entry requirements

Dos & Don'ts

Do Shake hands and introduce yourself when meeting someone for the first time.

Don't Talk about religion or politics. Things can get heated among those who share divergent views.

and visa guidelines before arriving.

➡ The US State Department (www.travel.state.gov) maintains the most comprehensive visa information, with lists of consulates and downloadable application forms.

➡ The Visa Waiver Program allows citizens of three dozen countries to enter the USA for stays of 90 days or less without first obtaining a US visa. See the ESTA website (https://esta.cbp.dhs.gov) for a current list. Under this program you must have a nonrefundable return ticket and 'e-passport' with digital chip.

➡ Visitors who don't qualify for the Visa Waiver Program need a visa. Basic requirements are a valid passport, recent photo, travel details and, often, proof of financial stability.

Behautz Behind the Scenes

Send Us Your Feedback

We love to hear from travelers – your comments help make our books better. We read every word, and we guarantee that your feedback goes straight to the authors. Visit **lonelyplanet.com/contact** to submit your updates and suggestions.

Note: We may edit, reproduce and incorporate your comments in Lonely Planet products such as guidebooks, websites and digital products, so let us know if you don't want your comments reproduced or your name acknowledged. For a copy of our privacy policy visit lonelyplanet.com/privacy.

Regis' Thanks

Countless people helped along the way, and I'm grateful to national park guides, lodging hosts, restaurant servers, barkeeps and baristas who shared tips and insight throughout South Florida. I'd also like to thank Cassandra and our daughters, Magdalena and Genevieve, who made the Miami trip all the more worthwhile.

Acknowledgements

Cover photograph: Vintage 1955 Chevrolet Bel Air automobile and cafes on Ocean Drive, Russell Kord/Alamy ©

Contents photograph: South Beach, Miami, Miami2you/Shutterstock ©

This Book

This 1st edition of Lonely Planet's *Pocket Miami* guidebook was researched and written by Regis St Louis. This guidebook was produced by the following:

Destination Editors Trisha Ping, Lauren Keith

Product Editors Genna Patterson, Grace Dobell

Senior Cartographer Alison Lyall

Book Designer Gwen Cotter

Assisting Editors Judith Bamber, Imogen Bannister, Melanie Dankel, Anita Isalska, Helen Koehne,

Rosie Nicholson, Kristin Odijk, Susan Paterson

Cover Researcher Marika Mercer

Thanks to Heather Champion, Jane Grisman, Corey Hutchison, Sandie Kestell, Gary Rafferty, Kathryn Rowan, Angela Tinson, Tony Wheeler

Index

See also separate subindexes for:

Eating p158
Drinking p158
Entertainment p158
Shopping p159

Sights 000
Map Pages **000**

Sights **000**
Map Pages **000**

Our Writers

Regis St Louis

Regis grew up in a small town in the American Midwest – the kind of place that fuels big dreams of travel – and he developed an early fascination with foreign dialects and world cultures. He spent his formative years learning Russian and a handful of Romance languages, which served him well on journeys across much of the globe. Regis has contributed to more than 50 Lonely Planet titles, covering destinations across six continents. His travels have taken him from the mountains of Kamchatka to remote island villages in Melanesia, and to many grand urban landscapes. When not on the road, he lives in New Orleans. Follow him on www.instagram.com/regisstlouis.

Published by Lonely Planet Global Limited
CRN 554153
1st edition – Jan 2018
ISBN 978 1 78657 7153
© Lonely Planet 2018   Photographs © as indicated 2018
10 9 8 7 6 5 4 3 2 1
Printed in Malaysia